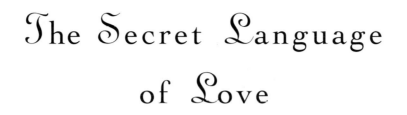

The Secret Language of Love

The Secret Language of Love

MEGAN TRESIDDER

*with paintings
by Emma Turpin*

CHRONICLE BOOKS
SAN FRANCISCO

The Secret Language of Love
Megan Tresidder

First published in the United States in 1997 by Chronicle Books

Copyright © 1997 by Duncan Baird Publishers
Text copyright © 1997 by Megan Tresidder
Illustrations and commissioned photographs copyright © 1997
by Duncan Baird Publishers
Paintings reproduced on pages 2, 5, 8, 18, 31, 39, 45, 50, 56,
76–7, 82, 85, 102, 118, 139, 153, 163, 169 © *Emma Turpin*
Cover design: *Jane Elizabeth Brown*
Cover image (front): *Lovers in a Yellow Sea* by Emma Turpin
Bird of Paradise (front): Detail from a piece of silk embroidery (18C.) from the Musée
Mobilier National, Paris
(Giraudon/Bridgeman Art Library, London)
Back cover image: Paris Bordone, *Pair of Lovers* (detail of Cupid), National Gallery, London

Editor: *Catherine Bradley*
Assistant Editor: *Slaney Begley*
Designers: *Gail Jones and Jeniffer Harte*
Commissioned Photography: *Richard McConnell*
Picture Research: *Julia Brown*
Indexer: *Drusilla Calvert*

for Simon

Library of Congress Cataloguing-in-Publication Data

Tresidder, Megan, 1958-
The secret language of love / by Megan Tresidder.
p. cm.
Includes bibliographical referencec and index.
ISBN 0-8118-1409-2 (hardcover). - - ISBN 0-8118-1433-5 (pk.)
1. Love. I. Title.
HO 801. T765   1997
306.7—dc20   96-10958
CIP

1 3 5 7 9 10 8 6 4 2

Typeset in Mrs Eaves
Font designed by *Zuzana Licko*
Colour reproduction by Colourscan, Singapore
Printed by Imago, Singapore

Distribution in Canada by
Raincoast Books
8680 Cambie Street
Vancouver, B.C. V6P 6M9

10 9 8 7 6 5 4 3 2 1

Chronicle Books
85 Second Street
San Francisco, CA 94105
Web Site: www. chronbooks.com

CONTENTS

118

ARCHETYPES OF LOVE

♡

172

BIBLIOGRAPHY

INDEX

175

ACKNOWLEDGMENTS

INTRODUCTION

O love is the crooked thing,
There is nobody wise enough
To find out all that is in it.

W. B. YEATS (1865—1939), "BROWN PENNY"

 Love is the most complex and important of all human emotions. It defies adequate definition, but in its grandeur and its imaginative power over our lives, it can be both creative and destructive, beautiful and terrifying. The barque of love can carry us to paradise, yet it can also leave us stranded in misery, mourning the loss of the closest relationship we will ever have with another human being.

Love is more than simply affection, although the same word is increasingly used for both emotions. It has many mysteries and many faces. An ascetic's yearning for the spirit of God or for an Absolute, the love between parents and children or brothers and sisters, the bond between two loving friends, the enduring contentment between a loving husband and wife long after sexual desire has ebbed, are all forms of deep love — some would say stronger and more permanent than romantic passion. For such loves, people have been willing to put their own interests second, even to sacrifice their lives, throughout history. To understand love, we need to look at all of these forms and at the mysterious connections and overlaps between them. However, at the core of this book, as at the centre of the human imagination, is erotic love.

From one point of view, all forms of true love are erotic if they involve longing. The Greek *eros*, or "passion-love", is the irresistible force that seals union, the powerful and unmistakably sexual desire to fuse with what we sense is missing. Such love renews itself with every generation, in spite of a vast literature of pessimism and tragedy. Unhappy love, frustrated love, doomed love or lost love are dominant themes of the novel, drama, classical ballet and opera; they have also been a recurring

Weddings in the 19th century followed an often long and formal period of courtship. This illustration from La mode illustrée *shows a bride having a dress fitting.*

favourite of the cinema. Religion, philosophy and psychology often seem to distrust the irresponsible wildness of passionate love, placing a higher value on more temperate personal relationships or a more diffused love for humankind, or for God.

Yet it is not difficult to see why passionate love has such a compelling attraction. It fascinates us because it promises a happiness that is not temperate but extraordinary — a state of being in which we not only sense that we have transcended the limits of self but also feel startlingly more alive. Under the influence of love the world around us looks completely different, its colours more vivid, the shapes of trees, flowers and leaves more three-dimensional. The air smells intoxicating. Blood sings in our veins. We float over the ground effortlessly. The mundane burdens of everyday life seem to be infinitely lighter. The sight and touch of the Other intoxicates us, and the thought of returning alone to an ordinary world is almost unbearable.

No such prosaic descriptions begin to capture the actual euphoria of falling in love. Some lyrical poetry comes close. Yet each love has its own secret language, making it near impossible to analyse or anatomize. In a real sense, love is like the spinning top described by Franz Kafka, which loses all its fascination when a hand stops it to examine what makes it work.

This book reviews some of the most significant ideas people have had about the nature of love through history, and identifies the fundamental archetypes that unconsciously influence our behaviour. It discusses the many facets of love and the ever-changing language of flirtation, courtship and fulfilment. Above all, however, it celebrates love as a magical transformation, erotic, passionate and romantic — the ephemeral beauty of the spinning top.

Modern love has grown out of a bewildering mixture of rituals, fashions, laws and customs. Philosophical theories and religious prohibitions or commandments have also contributed — as has a vast literature of role models. Compared with almost any other period in history, love has never been so liberated from social restrictions as it is now. Nor has it ever been undertaken with such casual ease.

This does not mean that it is any easier to fall in love or to sustain romantic passion today. The opposite may be true. The history of love has shown repeatedly that longing is positively increased by obstacles and delays, separations and rules of courtship. The steady removal of these rules during the 20th century has profoundly changed the nature of human relationships in the Western world.

Throughout the ages there has been fundamental disagreement not only about what makes us fall in love but also about whether the romantic concept of falling in love is "real love" at all. Another form of love has traditionally been placed higher in the moral scale. The Greeks called it *agape*, love for humankind. It is often linked with the ideal of Christian love because it looks beyond our own desires or needs toward the requirements of others.

The nobility of this form of love is indisputable. It coincides with what Christians see as the "gift love" of God, and it involves a conscious act of free will, a choice. Passionate love, on the other hand, seems to offer us no choice at all. It simply overwhelms us, rising suddenly and unbidden, welling up as an unconscious or instinctive force which we are powerless to resist. Eros was the Greek personification of this force. His advent has never been described more beautifully than by the poet of Lesbos, Sappho: "Love, looser of limbs, shakes me again, a sweet-bitter resistless creature."

The sexual content of *eros* has always been distrusted by philosophers, and is still distrusted by psychotherapists who have to deal with the problems that it creates. At times in the history of love, a rigid division has been drawn between *eros* and *agape*, as if sexual and selfless love could never be combined. In late medieval Europe, the Church looked to the teachings of St Paul, founded upon a profound distinction between spiritual and physical union. This anti-erotic view gave little encouragement in scripture to secular love; both virginity and chastity were praised above marriage, and no theologian successfully argued that passionate love could be an avenue to selfless or spiritual love.

The concept of courtly love, in which a lover would surrender his heart to his lady, first flourished in medieval France. Its influence survives today in many myths and romances, such as the Arthurian legends. In this tapestry from the 16th century, a suitor reads a love poem to his lady in a symbolic garden setting.

In this 15th-century Italian painting the triumph of the goddess Venus is being venerated by six legendary lovers: Achilles, Tristan, Lancelot, Samson, Paris and Troilus.

Although most world philosophies acknowledge that love is a multi-faceted emotion, the idea that erotic love was incompatible with spirituality was largely a medieval Western phenomenon. Eastern religions have long acknowledged that love can play an important role in spiritual happiness. Highly erotic carvings, such as depictions of the sexual exploits of Krishna and the *gopi* (milkmaid) Radha, decorate the façades of some Hindu temples, while the sexual and spiritual union of Shiva and Parvati became the basis of Tantric and Shakta philosophy.

In a period of new humanism, artists and writers of the European Renaissance swept away the idea that sexual love was inconsistent with sacred love. They described love between men and women as a joyous and transforming emotion, which in turn celebrated a divine, natural authority. The lovers featured in *I Modi*, an album of erotica engraved by Marcantonio Raimondi in 1524, are heroic participants in a pagan ritual. Titian's *Sacred and Profane Love* — a beautiful, if ironic, painting of the "higher" and "lower" forms of love — shows two Venuses, one representing an earthly force and the other a divine one. The artist depicted the divine Venus naked, the earthly one clothed, recognizing the erotic potential in concealment. This awareness now sustains an entire fashion industry, but despite such commercialism an innate respect for the beauty and power of human love continues to dominate our modern lives. Most modern writers on love believe that *eros* and *agape* are not only reconcilable, but that one can grow out of the other. Romantic love can develop into the loving friendship of mature love, still carrying the charge of passion that inspired it.

Titian's Sacred and Profane Love, *painted around 1515, is an ironic portrayal of the medieval belief that secular love is a second-rate emotion.*

The story of the Hindu god Krishna and the gopi (milkmaid) Radha is one of the greatest Indian romances. This painting depicts Krishna walking in a grove with his beloved Radha. In the bottom left, she tenderly anoints her lover's feet.

Two Lovers Listening to a Cuckoo, *by the 18th-century*
Japanese artist Ippitsusai Buncho, portrays the feeling of wonder
we have for everything around us when we are in love.

History shows that passionate love is a prize that is not easily won. At its heart is risk. Not only the risk of error or disappointment but of torment. Young lovers take the greatest risks of love not lasting because for them falling in love is often part of the whole process of self-discovery. Lawrence Durrell wrote about this aspect of love in his novel *Justine*: "Idle to imagine falling in love as a correspondence of minds, of thoughts; it is a simultaneous firing of two spirits involved in the autonomous act of growing up ... The loved object is simply one that has shared the same moment of time narcissistically; and the desire to be near the beloved object is not at first due to the idea of possessing it, but simply to let the two experiences compare themselves like reflections in different mirrors."

The idea of possessing the loved one comes later, and the risk of loss is then even more painful unless the lovers can move beyond self. Selfishness is always a component of falling in love. We want to adore another person — the kind of love that Aristotle felt was the most active and creative – but we also want to be adored ourselves. Not to have our love reciprocated is anguish enough. Being loved and then losing that love is agonizing. This is the "sweet-bitter" face of Eros that the poet Sappho described. Whatever else changes, it is love's mingling of joy and sorrow that will continue to haunt the human imagination.

In Western societies, many of the old restrictions and rigid codes of conduct were designed to protect women against giving birth to children outside the security of a "suitable" marriage. In changing the whole pattern of sexual relationships, safe contraception has inevitably altered patterns of love as well. Sometimes these changes are subtle. For example, the traditional rules of courtship, and clear distinctions between male and female roles in society, meant that lovers seldom had to sustain intimate relationships with each other before they were married. Instead, there was an interplay of closeness and separation, intimacy and distance. The separations enforced a degree of autonomy and independence which not only enabled desire to build up, but also maintained a degree of mystery between the sexes. One result of removing courtship restrictions and breaking down strict divisions between male and female spheres of life is that couples may be alone together much more than they were. Men have traditionally coped with this less well than women, and many continue to make periodic disappearances, both literal and emotional.

Such hurdles are far less obvious than the barriers with which previous generations had to contend. Surmounting them requires awareness and understanding of which physical and psychological differences between men and women are fundamental and which are not. This is not made easier by the fact that we are undergoing a remarkable revolution in attitudes toward gender. On every front, from the way that we dress to the jobs that we do, gender identity is being blurred. The drama of love is no longer played out by protagonists wearing distinctive costumes and performing traditional and clearly defined roles.

This illustration from the Roman de la Rose, painted around 1500, depicts a lady and her lover about to enter the garden of love.

This charming bas-relief, entitled A Basket of Loves, *depicts the goddess Venus releasing Cupids into the world.*

A much deeper change is the modern acceptance of the idea that passionate love can flourish within marriage or within a long-term relationship. Such expectations are in striking contrast to the often cynical views of the 18th century. "The French do not take pride in constancy," wrote Montesquieu, who thought that for a man to promise to love a woman for ever was as ridiculous as promising that he would always enjoy good health. Although today this seems a somewhat pessimistic view, at the time marriage was seen primarily as a financial contract. Weddings, especially those between aristocrats, were often arranged by the parents, and "love matches" were rare. Much earlier, the court romances of medieval Europe drew a clear distinction between the vows of love and marriage. The 12th-century noblewoman Marie, Comtesse de Champagne, wrote: "Love cannot extend its rights to married persons, for lovers give everything to each other without being forced in any way, as is not the case in marriage."

Eric Gill's illustration to Chaucer's Troilus and Cressida *portrays the couple in an embrace. There are no clues in the scene that soon Cressida will be unfaithful and shatter Troilus's illusions.*

Romantic love in the 19th century was thought to be compatible with marriage if minds and souls were perfectly attuned. To some extent, the less cynical modern belief that love can survive marriage, and indeed can grow stronger within it, was encouraged by better sex education and sexual awareness. In the openness of the "Sexual Revolution", skilled love-making was considered the key to lasting love. Accelerating divorce rates have subsequently cast doubt on such a simplistic view, and modern lovers generally believe that knowledge and mutual respect, rather than physical technique, form a stronger foundation for a relationship. Such cautiousness reveals a new approach to love, neither sceptical nor starry-eyed. If it is true that a new vision of love is forming under the pressure of rapid social changes in the 20th century, it can only be built on an understanding of the past. The links between sex, love and the changing moods of the human heart remain mysterious, and traditional philosophy, mythology and literature still have much to teach us about love in all its possible manifestations.

THE ANATOMY OF LOVE

Hot beautiful furless animals
Played in a clearing opened by their desire.

THOM GUNN, "ADULTERY"

Thom Gunn's image of lovers as animals playing tells us more about how love came into the world than whole books of intellectual theory. Where our deepest, least definable emotions are concerned, we turn to poets and artists to give them vivid expression and shape. Whatever psychologists or biologists may tell us about the subject, no true anatomy of love can ignore either the primal force of desire or humanity's unique capacity for aesthetic pleasure. It is this capacity, manifested through imagination, idealism and play, that works upon mere instinct and transforms it into something different and marvellous.

Philosophy has always assumed an important role in deciphering the mysteries of love. Some of the most imaginative and influential theories are contained in Plato's *Symposium*, written in the 4th century BC. His definition of love as "the desire and pursuit of the whole" has often been reinterpreted, but never bettered.

THE GENESIS OF LOVE

Scientific theories of the origin of love look back far beyond the sophistication of civilized romance. Zoologists who have compared the evolution and behaviour of humans and animals think that love began as an advanced form of the strong pair-bonding also seen in primates. Like humans, primates have a long period of dependency on their parents. Such long "childhoods" profoundly influence our emotional ability to form close relationships and to love.

Forces of evolution are also thought by some scientists to play an unconscious role in our selection of a mate. This view appeared even before biology began to focus on the "selfish gene". The 19th-century German philosopher Arthur Schopenhauer said that the "genius of the species" persuades us to serve the next generation under the delusion that we are making ourselves happy. Love ensures that we reproduce and is an emotion inseparable from sex, he thought. The emotion leads us to search for someone perfectly attuned to our own personality, but remains in essence an individualized sexual impulse, however ethereal.

The Bible story of Adam and Eve is shown in this 12th-century Spanish painting. God makes Eve from Adam's rib. Their love is innocent until they taste the forbidden fruit and are banished from the garden of Eden.

More recent study of the emotion of love as a complex series of chemical reactions has made little progress. It is hard enough to distinguish chemically between the adrenaline built up by desire and that generated by stress. Showing that love is chemically different from sexual yearning is beyond the current capabilities of laboratory science. Yet everything tells us that the two states of mind are not the same and that the difference is crucial.

If, as Schopenhauer believed, nature added an emotion to a purely physical act, how marvellously the human animal has developed it! This is perhaps what the French author Honoré de Balzac meant when he wrote: "Love is the poetry of the senses. It is the key to all that is great in man's destiny. It is sublime or it is nothing. How blasphemous it is to use the word 'love' in connection with the reproduction of the species."

Paul Gauguin's watercolour Te Nave Nave, *painted on the island of Tahiti, exemplifies a common male fantasy — that of a beautiful young woman, innocent yet inviting.*

THE MEETING OF SOULS

Swans appear frequently in myths, where they are often revealed to be bewitched humans. Apart from their great beauty, this may be because they are one of the few members of the animal kingdom to mate for life.

"I cannot live without my soul," cries lost Heathcliff in *Wuthering Heights*, inconsolable after the death of Catherine Earnshaw. Behind Emily Brontë's novel of kindred spirits haunted and tormented by separation lies a long tradition of Western and Eastern mysticism in which love is centred in the soul.

Plato's *Symposium*, written in the 4th century BC, first described love as a longing for union with an unconscious, ideal image. In this conception of love, Eros embodies a purely spiritual desire. Response to the external beauty of an individual body is caused by the soul's natural affinity for perfection rather than through any sexual impulse.

The Platonic concept of soul love has influenced ideas in both Christian and Muslim societies for centuries. To the medieval mind, it perfectly explained why sexual fulfilment still left the heart yearning, the soul unfulfilled. Themes of spiritual union dominated Islamic love poetry. This "higher" form of love was also celebrated by the great poets of the Italian Renaissance, Dante and Petrarch. The latter described his inspiration Laura in terms of religious adoration: she was "the source of that uplifting grace which guides us by the proper path to Heaven".

The notion of souls loving for all eternity was revived as a literary theme in the 19th century and since then it has never entirely disappeared. In its most extreme form the elevation of the soul above the body led to the ideal of lovers preferring a joint death to the consummation of their passion. The more humanist perspective is that perfect love integrates body and soul.

In this Indian miniature of the 18th century, a prince
and his lover are shown cocooned in their own world, in flight from reality.

THE LONGING FOR UNION

In nearly all myths of creation, the primal state involves a single, total principle. This may be a god, a cosmic ocean, pure Self or the force of chaos, but the original being in each case must divide itself to produce the diversity of living things. For centuries sexual desire and longing were believed to arise from the separation of an originally bisexual or androgynous entity. For example, in Indian myth the creator god Brahma forces the divine Shiva, half-male, half-female, to expel his female side, Parvati. She slips back into him after cunningly replicating herself as a female deity, whereupon Shiva falls in love with the Parvati double.

Like most myths, that of the androgyne is full of biological and psychological insights. In the 20th century the psychologist Carl Jung identified the "anima" and "animus" as the female and male archetypes buried within all human psyches. He believed that elements of the opposite sex are deeply embedded in our unconscious, recalling the bisexuality of a newly conceived human embryo.

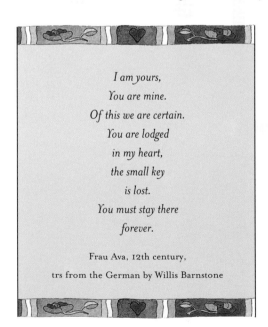

I am yours,
You are mine.
Of this we are certain.
You are lodged
in my heart,
the small key
is lost.
You must stay there
forever.

Frau Ava, 12th century,
trs from the German by Willis Barnstone

Plato jokingly used the myth of the androgyne to explain the different forms of physical love in his famous *Symposium*. Speaking through the playwright Aristophanes, he claimed that there were three original sexes, all with double faces, limbs and organs. The doubles were either male-female, male-male or female-female until the god Zeus, annoyed at their insolent self-confidence, split them down the middle. Ever since, anguished men and women have sought their missing halves, either heterosexual or homosexual. The search for love is a fundamental yearning to be reunited, to lose the separate self in the Other. The reason that some pairings continue to leave us dissatisfied is that we have not found the perfect match.

Plato's comical story does contain an essential truth about human love — that it is in part a longing to escape our sense of insufficiency. The Romantic poet Samuel Taylor

In Marc Chagall's Quai des Célestins *the woman's body is more distinct than the man's, which envelops her in a protective shadow. The lithograph reflects our basic need to merge with the one we love.*

Coleridge described the emotion as "a desire of the whole being to be united to some thing or some being felt necessary to its completeness, by the most perfect means that nature permits". The experience of love is often infused with a longing that is close to nostalgia. It is almost as if we do have a presentiment that in some earlier life we experienced a complete love.

25

EROTIC LOVE

The link between sex and love is so powerful that the word "erotic" has become synonymous with the arousal of sexual desire. In our own times, Eros appears to be restricted to physical passion, balanced on a knife-edge between desire and fulfilment. For, as the literature of unhappy love reveals, sexual fulfilment can paradoxically extinguish desire. The greatest intensity of erotic love may therefore occur in the moment before desire achieves its object.

The belief that Eros — in the sense of pure physical desire — consists of a longing for something beyond reach is perfectly evoked in John Keats' famous "Ode on a Grecian Urn": "More happy love! more happy, happy love! / Forever warm and still to be enjoyed, / Forever panting, and forever young."

The happy love is embodied by a maiden, placed just beyond her lover's grasp in a scene painted on the urn. This instant before union is firmly fixed in time and therefore protected from the changing seasons of love experienced in the real world.

The paradox that desire, like hunger, can disappear when physically satisfied has preoccupied writers from many diverse cultures. Plato's solution was to give desire a spiritual dimension, which effectively placed a far greater distance between love and its final object. The consummation of sexual passion became only a stage on the way to a higher goal, allowing love itself to persist as a sense of unassuaged longing.

The ebb and flow of desire can possess an emotional as well as a physical aspect. The French writer Simone Weil has described the tortuous fluctuations of human love, in which love can diminish when we are most adored: "All our desires are contradictory, like the desire for food. I want the person I love to love me. However, if he is totally devoted to me he does not exist any longer and I cease to love him. And as long as he is not totally devoted to me, he does not love me enough. Hunger and repletion."

The passion of the god Krishna and his cow-herdess love Radha is one of the most erotic tales in Hindu literature. It has been the inspiration for many painted miniatures.

Below: *The* Private Pleasure of Emperor Jahangir *features a pair of lovers in a romantic garden setting. Virility and sexual prowess were considered positive attributes in a ruler.*

26

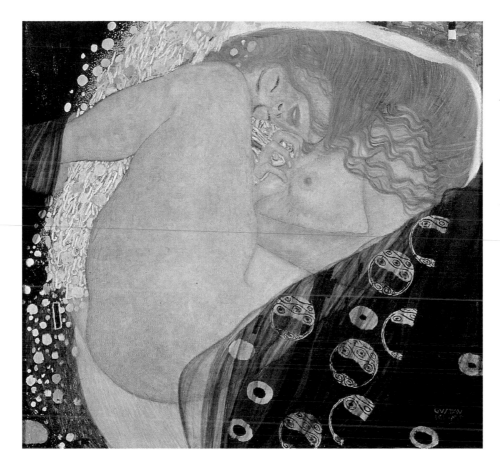

Gustav Klimt's volupt-
uous painting **Danaë**
tells the story of the
princess of Argos, whose
father imprisoned her in
a bronze tower after an
oracle foretold that a son
of hers would kill him.
She was visited by Zeus in
the form of a shower of
gold, and later gave birth
to a son, Perseus.

Erotic love is essentially a maelstrom of conflicting impulses and sensations. Sex is an integral part, of course, but cannot be considered its ultimate object. If this were so, people who continue to make each other happy sexually would have no reason to fall out of love — but there is plenty of evidence that they often do. Pure lust, although sometimes confused with the infatuation stage of love, is a much less challenging, easily comprehended emotion. It is quite possible to have a great loveless sex affair. Indeed the Roman philosopher and poet Lucretius pointed out in the 1st century BC that love may actually distract from sensual pleasure. The bittersweet complexity of erotic love stems from the fact that it is precariously focused on a single person and calls into play an infinite number of wishes, needs and obscure desires, all charged with the high explosive of sex.

This ancient Greek red-
figure cup is decorated
with the lovers Ariadne
and Dionysus, accompa-
nied by the god Eros. The
story of Ariadne, who
was abandoned and
rescued before finding
happiness, shows the
complexities and dangers
of erotic love.

27

THE PSYCHOLOGY OF LOVE

Love is the most poetic emotion that we know, and at the same time one of our most basic needs. Its associated emotions, experiences and fantasies are delineated in the myths and fairytales of innumerable societies and cultures, yet its causes and impact still escape our full comprehension. It has been mocked as a transient illusion ("a gross exaggeration of the difference between one person and another," quipped George Bernard Shaw), and celebrated as a blind, biological imperative — the expression of an immensely powerful life force.

The idea of love as a biological drive provided a starting point for the revolutionary theories of Sigmund Freud. His psychology of love was grounded in the belief that the role of the *libido,* operating at the unconscious level of animal instinct, had been vastly underestimated in identifying both the source of love and the seemingly mysterious process by which we select a love object.

Freud was the first to propose a coherent theory of love based on scientific principles. He concluded that we fall in love because we follow rules buried below the level of our conscious thought. Psychoanalysis seemed to reveal that these rules were derived from our infancy and in particular from our sensual attachment to those who loved us — or who did not love us, although we longed for them to do so.

This suggestion came as a shock to contemporary society, which found it hard to accept that children's love for their parents could have a significant sensual basis. Freud's theories, put forward almost a hundred years ago, have been attacked ever since, and much modified by his disciples. Yet he remains the most original psychologist of the 20th century, and the most influential.

Freud is criticized for overemphasizing the role of instinct (the *id*), and therefore of sexual drives as a whole.

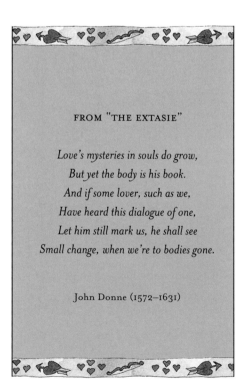

FROM "THE EXTASIE"

Love's mysteries in souls do grow,
But yet the body is his book.
And if some lover, such as we,
Have heard this dialogue of one,
Let him still mark us, he shall see
Small change, when we're to bodies gone.

John Donne (1572–1631)

The biblical story of the temptation of Adam and Eve has long been used to condemn female desire. Eve's lack of restraint is seen as the cause of Man's fall from grace, while the serpent who tempted Eve to accept the forbidden fruit is often depicted with a woman's head and torso.

This detail of The World Before the Flood, *from Hieronymus Bosch's* The Garden of Earthly Delights *(c.1505), depicts a world full of strange lusts and pleasures.*

However, his preoccupation with the *id* was understandable in a society which attempted to repress sexual desire, especially in women. Freud tried to redress the balance by insisting that sex was a primary instinct in both men and women and a major component of erotic love. He defined Eros as a longing for union — the *libido* mingling sexual and emotional desires.

The interdependence of male and female needs was perceived many

Many modern psychologists believe that our psychosexual identity contains male and female aspects, and that they play some part in determining with whom we fall in love. The importance of the first few years of life is also now thought to be considerable. In relationships as adults we tend to seek a replacement for the love and attention once experienced in childhood — perhaps accounting for the almost magical, absolute certainty with which lovers often seem to recognize one another.

The psychologists who followed Freud have been able to draw upon a far greater knowledge of biochemistry. Yet this has tended to work against the idea that the mystery of love can be explained by genes or hormones. Clinical studies seem to show the opposite — that, to an overwhelming degree, our love relationships are culturally determined.

Biological functions may provide a basis for erotic desire, but the influence of social expectations and cultural values is enormous. Sexuality itself is hugely influenced by these factors. Many psychologists believe that we begin forming neurophysical "love-maps" very early in our lives. People who have developed the idea in childhood that they are girls and not boys (or *vice versa*) are often unable to change their "mind-maps" in spite of physical evidence to the contrary.

In Greek mythology the maiden Atalanta swore only to marry a man who could run faster than herself. She was finally beaten by the cunning Milanion, who threw three golden apples in front of her which she stopped to pick up.

centuries before Freud. In Chinese philosophy the whole universe is infused with the opposing yet complementary powers of *yin* and *yang*, representing essential female and male qualities. The ancient symbol for *yin* and *yang* epitomizes their mutual dependence — two perfectly integrated halves unite to form a complete, harmonious circle.

Emma Turpin's powerful vision of a mother and her children also represents the conflicting impulses within a woman. The passionate girl struggling to be free is balanced by the pragmatic conformist. Love affairs often serve to focus the tensions inherent in women's lives

They may be driven to change their gender physically, in order to fit their perceived sexual identity.

Falling in love involves an often contradictory mixture of sexual desire, emotions and values. The paradoxes of love swiftly become apparent: a longing for closeness contends with the need to assert our own identity, and erotic desire itself is episodic. The need to experience a sense of power in a relationship — and yet also have the confidence to surrender control — fluctuates from day to day, and is reflected in the seemingly inconsistent behaviour of a couple when viewed by those on the outside. It is our ability to balance these diverse psychosexual demands that determines the success or otherwise of our love relationships.

We need to idealize our love choice, not only sexually but also in the sphere of culture, aesthetics and morality. At its best, love promotes an imaginative empathy with its object which transcends the individual ego and creates a unique sense of harmony with the outside world. For most people, despite — or even because of — its many contradictions and difficulties, love is still an emotion to be valued above all else.

This illustration comes from a manual of social etiquette for women, written in the 15th century by Christine de Pisan.

Since we through war awhile must part

Sweetheart, and learn to lose

Daily use

Of all that satisfied our heart:

Lay up those secrets and those powers

Wherewith you pleased and cherished me these two years:

Now we must draw, as plants would,

On tubers stored in a better season,

Our honey and heaven;

Only our love can store such food.

Is this to make a god of absence?

A new-born monster to steal our sustenance?

We cannot quite cast out lack and pain.

Let him remain — what he may devour

We can well spare:

He never can tap this, the true vein.

I have no words to tell you what you were,

But when you are sad, think, Heaven could give no more.

Anne Ridler, "At Parting"

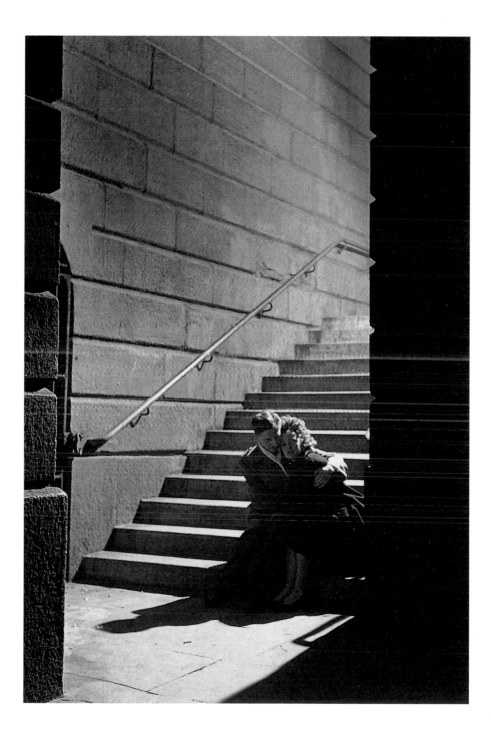

There is a strong wall about me to protect me:
It is built of the words you have said to me.

There are swords about me to keep me safe:
They are the kisses of your lips.

Before me goes a shield to guard me from harm:
It is the shadow of your arms between me and danger.

All the wishes of my mind know your name,
And the white desires of my heart
They are acquainted with you.
The cry of my body for completeness,
That is a cry to you.
My blood beats out your name to me, unceasing, pitiless
Your name, your name.

Mary Carolyn Davies, "Love Song"

LOVE AND BEAUTY

The swiftest cue for love has always been human beauty, striking with the speed and force of an arrow and bringing the strongest of us to our knees. The relationship between love and perceived beauty has been celebrated in widely different cultures for centuries. Islamic love poetry is devoted almost exclusively to the praise of ideal beauty, whilst the art of Hindu temples is peopled with divinely beautiful figures symbolizing love. In the ancient Greek pantheon, Aphrodite is the goddess of beauty as well as love.

This Indian miniature shows Krishna outside the chamber of love, preparing to shoot his beloved Radha with the flaming arrow of desire.

The Three Graces, shown below in a painting by Raphael, were the hand-maidens of Aphrodite, the Greek goddess of love. Like their mistress, they personified beauty, charm and grace.

As a motive for love, beauty is much less popular with rationalists. Voltaire, for example, ridiculed its absurd premise in his play *Candide*: the hero's passionate love for the beautiful Cunégonde is thwarted for such a long time that when he finally marries her she has become both bad-tempered and hideous.

The obvious and sensible argument that other qualities are more lasting has little effect on anyone who has ever fallen in love. Beauty creates a hunger; our recognition that it is ephemeral makes it all the more heartbreaking and desirable.

Male beauty is also a powerful catalyst for romantic love. Hippolyte Flandrin's Young Man on a Rock *(c. 1830) portrays a pensive youth, apparently unaware of his charms.*

Lovers can know in their hearts that the beautiful one they embrace is flawed — yet be unable to give them up, as W.H. Auden confessed: "But in my arms till break of day / Let the living creature lie / Mortal, guilty, but to me / The entirely beautiful."

Beauty is a dangerous gift, both for the beautiful and for those who love them. Beautiful people often feel that they are not loved for themselves and that because of this they will be deserted as their beauty fades. They may also be narcissistic or egotistical — though by no means always. Our ideas of beauty are peculiarly subjective, responding to expressive qualities of personality and character as well as contemporary fashion and taste. A lover's capacity to idealize the Beloved can paradoxically accompany a clear perception of their physical faults. Perfect beauty may sometimes appear an inscrutable mask; blemishes may be precisely what touch the heart of someone in love. Once we are experiencing love for a real person an abstract physical ideal becomes much less relevant. Beauty certainly inspires love, but cannot alone keep it.

LOVE AND VIRTUE

Portraits such as this one of a man and wife reflected the 16th-century belief that a good and honourable marriage would be wealthy and fruitful. These qualities are symbolized by the woman's gold chain and the lemons respectively.

The idea of loving someone for their admirable moral qualities is something that we associate more with 19th-century earnestness than with modern concepts of romantic love. Yet modern psychology is beginning to remind us that successful love needs the person whom we love to share our own ideals, or even to inspire us to be better than we are.

Erotic love and moral virtue have not always been seen as natural bedfellows.

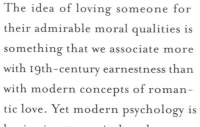

In the Islamic faith, as well as in many pagan traditions, secular love was seen as an ennobling emotion, able at its best to inspire artistic creativity, courage and devotion. This belief also lay behind the famous medieval idea of courtly love. However, in the early Christian Church the only pure love was considered to be the love of God, and in the 12th century the "Song of Songs", the Bible's sole poem cele-

brating the power and sweetness of erotic love, was even interpreted as an allegory of the Virgin Mary.

The religious reformer Martin Luther acknowledged the force of sexual desire and rejected the idea that marriage was an state inferior to chastity. For centuries, however, both Protestant and Catholic doctrine maintained that it was virtuous to keep physical passion strictly within the bounds of social duty: intemperate erotic love was viewed as a morally destructive weakness.

The distance between love and virtue narrowed dramatically in the 19th century. Marrying for love began to be widely, though not universally, accepted, and poets such as the atheistic Shelley wrote of love as a heightening of moral sensibility. The philosopher John Stuart Mill believed that an ideal marriage should involve an ethical education of like-minded individuals: "each can enjoy the luxury of looking up to the other, and can have ... the pleasure of leading and being led."

By the end of the 19th century, married love had been virtually deified. These elevated beliefs may have been a strain to live up to, but, even for people

This Chantilly enamel box of the 18th century is decorated with a sedate couple in bed. The union of marriage was seen as a source of civic virtue as well as of personal happiness and wellbeing.

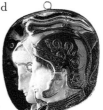

Throughout the ages, jewelry has been given and worn by lovers as a pledge of constancy or commitment. This cameo of a royal couple dates from the 3rd century BC.

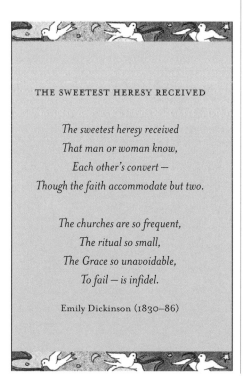

who were not deeply religious, marriage was seen as a solemn and binding commitment.

The great change in the 20th century is that physical passion no longer needs the sanctity of marriage to be virtuous. It is rather one aspect of a shared ideal, through which two people may transcend the everyday world. Whether modern love lasts or not is less a matter of law or religion than of continuing mutual love and respect — which now depends, perhaps more than ever, on the personal virtue of each partner.

Modern codes of love have changed the ways in which we view everyday behaviour. In former times the fiery, desirable woman in this painting by Emma Turpin might have been seen as a seductress, but to modern eyes she represents a benevolent, protective force.

THE SWEETEST HERESY RECEIVED

The sweetest heresy received
That man or woman know,
Each other's convert —
Though the faith accommodate but two.

The churches are so frequent,
The ritual so small,
The Grace so unavoidable,
To fail — is infidel.

Emily Dickinson (1830–86)

LOVE AND FRIENDSHIP

The time-honoured protestation that someone is not a lover but "just a good friend" seems to reveal a vast gulf between the two conditions. However, as many of us proceed to discover, this mutable and ambivalent boundary may be both possible and pleasurable to cross. The "marriage of true minds", celebrated by Shakespeare in one of his great love sonnets, lies at the core of our deepest friendships, and has often been perceived as one of the noblest causes of love. Mental affinity may not capture the heart as swiftly as beauty, but it can nevertheless provide the basis for deep love — and passion can develop from it.

The delicate balance between the emotional commitment of friendship and acknowledgment of love has been a source of fascination for centuries. Sigmund Freud believed that latent sexual impulses always underlie intense friendship, which he once described as a "state of evenly suspended, steadfast

Pellizza Da Volpede's delightful painting Lovers Walking *captures the intimate moments of friendship in love.*

affectionate feeling, which has little external resemblance any more to the stormy agitations of genital love, from which it nevertheless derived". Yet other cultures, both ancient and modern, have praised friendship as the purest, least selfish form of love. Many 19th-century writers, drawn together by their craft, formed relationships involving all the intensity that we associate with love. It is too simplistic merely to assign a sexual motive to the creative intimacy of Flaubert and Turgenev, Wordsworth and Coleridge, Byron and Shelley. Guy de Maupassant wrote of Flaubert and Turgenev, who corresponded for many years and who waited with impatience for their various meetings, "These men love each other in a fraternal friendship."

Non-sexual friendship between men and men, women and women or men and women can create emotional bonds as strong as all but the most intense forms of erotic love — and often more

enduring. Byron, who described erotic love as "a sort of hostile transaction", believed that men and women made excellent friends if they were not lovers. Yet a really happy physical relationship tells us that friendship and sensuality can be combined — and must be if it is to last. A true friendship, according to 19th-century Romantics, is a deep spiritual and emotional affinity: a tie of mutual sympathy, without which neither friendship nor love will endure.

Picnic in May, *a 19th-century painting by Szinyei Merse Pal, depicts the elements of flirtation that are present in most deep friendships between men and women.*

41

ILLUSION AND REALITY

In the early 20th century the worlds of advertising and marketing became increasingly influential in determining how people saw themselves and others. Frans Masereel's woodcut of a man gazing at the mannequins in a shop window shows how people may fall in love with a plastic ideal.

"Love is the son of deceit and father of illusion," wrote the Spanish scholar Miguel de Unamuno in *The Tragic Sense of Life* (1913). Such an anguished disbelief in the reality of love is probably shared by anyone who has suddenly and inexplicably stopped loving another, or has been betrayed by someone they thought cared for them.

The sometimes ephemeral nature of erotic love may indeed enable cynics to dismiss the whole emotion as an illusion. If real, how can it possibly disappear in the blink of an eye? Infatuations that depend purely on physical chemistry are particularly prone to sudden evaporation. If physical desire wanes, or if other values begin to influence the relationship, coldness or dislike can follow with disconcerting speed.

In Hinduism even lasting love is regarded as one aspect of *maya*, or illusion. The world – and everything in it – was formed from the creative power of *maya*, and so human love, in some ways our deepest, most vain attachment to the world of the senses, is always tinged with an awareness of its ephemeral nature. Nevertheless, love is as "real" as any other human construct. To say, as Shakespeare does in *A Midsummer Night's Dream*, "The lunatic, the lover and the poet, are of imagination all compact", does not invalidate the reality of lunacy, love or poetry. Love is not only an emotion, but also a human quality, as impossible to deny as are truthfulness or courage. Its consequences may well be short-lived or unpredictable, but they are also dramatic, visible and real.

The story of Cupid and Psyche (see page 54) illustrates how, despite the fascination of a dream lover, we eventually need to know his or her true identity. If love is to endure, it must be able to withstand the demands of the daylight world.

Stendhal likened falling in love to a transforming process of crystallization. "Visitors to the mines at Salzburg," he wrote, "are in the habit of throwing bare, wintry twigs into the depths of the cavern; two or three months later, when these are withdrawn, they are found to be covered by sparkling crystals."

Despite the fragility of the crystals and the imagination's role in sustaining them, Stendhal considers love to be far from illusory. On the contrary, it is the only reality: "The soul has forged its ideal, and whenever it meets this model in the flesh, the work of crystallization begins."

We may often fall in love under the spell of a self-created vision. In Flaubert's novel, Emma Bovary's fascination with the idle philanderer Rodolphe is no less intense for having been founded on fantasy: "a phantom composed of her most passionate memories, her most enjoyable books, and her strongest desires". Sharpened by imagination, her love soon disintegrates in the cold light of experience. Fantasies of love in the real world are often similarly inclined to evaporate if analyzed.

The mirror is a traditional symbol of love and beauty. Robert Anning Bell's delightful Cupid's Mirror *shows how the images we have of ourselves and the world around can be almost magically transformed when we fall in love.*

The initial stages of a love affair may be sustained largely through illusion, although few would relinquish its early euphoria on that account. Love is far more than "falling in love", however. It may be not only the accretion described by Stendhal, but also a stripping away of illusion to acknowledge and love the fallible human within. It is this kind of clear-sighted, honest love that provides, for many people, the most "real" and enduring experience in life.

LOVE AND LONELINESS

On the Tiles,
a woodcut by Eric Gill, illustrates
our instinct to curl up and hide when
we feel isolated.

The human need to escape from solitude is intimately linked with love in many mythologies. According to the Bible's Book of Genesis, Eve was created to reduce Adam's isolation, which was recognized as a condition that impoverished the spirit: "It is not good that man should be alone." The story of Adam's and Eve's expulsion from Eden has been described as a psychological allegory of our sense of isolation from the natural world — the knowledge that we are separated man from woman and that we must all finally face death alone. The more people mature and develop their own sense of individuality, the more acutely is loneliness experienced. Love affairs are often sought to avoid solitude, yet the greatest isolation of all may be encountered in the final, faltering stages of a relationship. The special intensity of first love may in part be a response to the sudden miracle of sensual intimacy. So overwhelming is this that parting from each other even for an hour, let alone for a period of days, becomes virtually unbearable. It is as if part of ourself is being dragged away from us. In an established relationship, being apart is never quite the same as the feeling of loneliness, as we continue to feel the presence of the beloved in an almost physical way. If a lover is lost permanently, the sense of renewed loneliness can be devastating.

Consciously or not, our human need to escape loneliness is always a part of loving someone — which is not to say that love removes the need. Those who love the most intensely are often the loneliest, suffering most from absences, misunderstandings, betrayals, or the eventual loss of love. This is another of love's bittersweet paradoxes. We often feel that we would die without the beloved. Yet to achieve a successful, lasting relationship, we must also discover how to survive alone.

The fear of loneliness can set limits on our
emotional growth. Once we have the strength to survive on our
own, we can exercise more choice in a relationship. This painting
by Emma Turpin shows a woman alone, gathering fruit and
flowers from an otherwise barren landscape.

Tonight I can write the saddest lines.

Write, for example, 'The night is shattered
and the blue stars shiver in the distance.'

The night wind revolves in the sky and sings.

Tonight, I can write the saddest lines.
I loved her, and sometimes she loved me too.

Through nights like this one, I held her in my arms.
I kissed her again and again under the endless sky.

She loved me, sometimes I loved her too.
How could one not have loved her great still eyes.

Tonight I can write the saddest lines.
To think that I do not have her. To feel that I have lost her.

To hear the immense night, still more immense without her.
And the verse falls to the soul like dew to the pasture.

What does it matter that my love could not keep her.
The night is shattered and she is not with me.

This is all. In the distance someone is singing. In the distance.
My soul is not satisfied that it has lost her.

Pablo Neruda (1904–73), "The Saddest Lines",

trs from the Spanish by W. S. Merwin

First time he kissed me, he but only kissed
The fingers of this hand wherewith I write,
And ever since it grew more clean and white, ..
Slow to world-greetings .. quick with its "Oh, list,"
When the angels speak. A ring of amethyst
I could not wear here plainer to my sight,
Than that first kiss. The second passed in height
The first, and sought the forehead, and half missed,
Half falling on the hair. O beyond meed!
That was the chrism of love, which love's own crown,
With sanctifying sweetness, did precede.
The third, upon my lips, was folded down
In perfect, purple state! since when, indeed,
I have been proud and said, "My Love, my own."

Elizabeth Barrett Browning (1806–61), "Sonnet from the Portuguese XXXVIII"

DIMENSIONS OF THE HEART

I am two fooles, I know

For loving, and for saying so

In whining Poetry;

But where's that wiseman, that would not be I,

If she would not deny?

JOHN DONNE (1573–1631), "THE TRIPLE FOOLE"

Writers may argue about the origin of love, but none disputes the bewildering range of its emotional scale. Being in love may produce our greatest happiness but, in the words of the prose-poem "Deirdre" by James Stephens, it is also sometimes "savagery in the blood, and pain in the bone, and greed and despair in the mind. It is to be thirsty in the night and unslaked in the day. It is to carry memory like a thorn in the heart. It is to drip one's blood as one walks."

Love has infinite moods and forms, and several different ages, from the serenity of enduring commitment to the overwhelming beauty of youthful love, when the sensory world pours in upon us and changes everything. The search for lasting love is always uncertain: passion may be unrequited, or betrayed, or simply eroded by time, yet in its tumultuous impact love reveals the most surprising dimensions of the human heart.

SYMPTOMS OF LOVE

So remarkable are the symptoms of lovesickness that they were considered in medieval Europe to be a physical or mental malady to which the noble-born (by implication, the more sensitive) were particularly prone. Classic symptoms of the yearning lover included sleeplessness, nightmares, hallucinations, pallor, lack of concentration and loss of appetite. A manic elation might be succeeded by extreme misery and a hopeless feeling that the adored one was a paragon of beauty and virtue far beyond reach. These effects were compounded by physical sensations of breathlessness and a pounding heart. A languid demeanour and piteous sighs became a form of medieval courtship which any self-respecting lover felt obliged to display — although they were surely also faked by shrewd philanderers to counterfeit sincerity.

This Persian manuscript shows two lovers totally absorbed in each other.

Lovers, of course, have always believed that their sickness can only be cured by the responsive presence of the beloved. However, through history a range of remedies has been proposed, from the pragmatic to the absurd. In the 11th century Constantine's *Viaticum* claimed that Eros was a disease of men's brains, and recommended recourse to prostitutes as a means of calming the inflammation. Priests, summoned to restore the lover's mental equilibrium, advised less radical cures, such as travel, sport, games, better food, plenty of wine and regular bathing and sleeping. Magnetism, microbes and astronomical influences were suspected causes of lovesickness in the 17th century, and as late as 1904 Dr Charles Féré compared the impact of love at first sight to an electric shock or spasm — a sensation similar to that felt by water diviners.

Modern research into the chemistry of rapture does reveal a correlation between high levels of neurotransmitters and the mood swings of lovesick romantics. Injections of adrenaline can induce similar symptoms of physical arousal — a pounding heart, trembling knees and

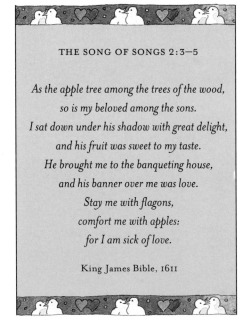

THE SONG OF SONGS 2:3–5

As the apple tree among the trees of the wood,
so is my beloved among the sons.
I sat down under his shadow with great delight,
and his fruit was sweet to my taste.
He brought me to the banqueting house,
and his banner over me was love.
Stay me with flagons,
comfort me with apples:
for I am sick of love.

King James Bible, 1611

 hands, flushing and sweating — revealing that emotions are not so much alternative forms of psychological stress as different interpretations of it. Self-delusion also plays a considerable role in our experience of love's symptoms. Attraction to another may be sublimated into a defensive antagonism, or hastily dismissed by the person who feels it as "mere" infatuation. The impulse of love is closely linked with that of sexual desire, and only after disentangling the confusion can we decide if we are "in love" or not.

Even if we recognize the symptoms of love, our immediate reaction is unpredictable. In the presence of someone for whom we feel an instant physical attraction, we may feel suddenly tongue-tied, clumsy and excruciatingly shy. More sophisticated lovers, however, will seek to respond to such an encounter by displaying a sudden and dazzling amount of poise and wit.

In Matisse's painting La Rève (The Dream) *a woman lies naked on her bed, thinking longingly about her absent lover.*

FIRST LOVE

This Renaissance painting, attributed to G.B. Bertucci, depicts Daphnis and Chloë, two foundlings brought up by shepherds, who gradually fall in love.

For all the strong and complex passions that it arouses, love has a child-like side. In acquiring sexual experience, there is always some nostalgia for the loss of innocence, some longing for love to continue as a spirit pure and delicate as air.

Parents often project this longing on to their adolescent children, wishing young lovers to remain suspended on the wings of love in a kind of ethereal bliss. The perfect archetype of this yearning is the story of Cupid and Psyche, told by the Roman writer, Apuleius, in the 2nd century AD. Having aroused the jealousy of the goddess Venus by her great beauty, Psyche is visited each night by a gentle, sweet-smelling bridegroom whose identity she is forbidden to know. Her evil sisters persuade Psyche to spy upon her lover while he is asleep. Her lamp reveals the beautiful form of the winged god Cupid, one of whose arrows pricks her as she plays with it, drawing blood. He wakes and flees when burning oil from the lamp falls on his shoulder. Yet the story ends happily: after she has completed a series of dangerous trials, Psyche is rescued by Cupid from a death-like-trance. Although born mortal, Psyche is eventually permitted to join the gods and marry her lover.

Cupid and Psyche seem to represent an almost unisexual couple — a romantic vision of young lovers who in their graceful and delicate sensuality are almost mirror-images of one another. In Antonio Canova's famous sculpture, Cupid's body is almost as feminine as Psyche's.

The American scholar Jean Hagstrum has suggested that the idea of delicate love may anticipate "an influential modern idea that to feminize life may in fact be to civilize it". The story of Cupid and Psyche may perhaps be interpreted as an allegory of young lovers finding that they are not frighteningly different from each other.

FIRST LOVE

In Amity, *a painting by Bernard Fleetwood Walker,*
the friendship of two young adolescents is gently tinted by their
burgeoning sexuality.

55

LOVE'S HESITATIONS

This Elizabethan miniature by Nicholas Hilliard shows a tormented young man in a rose garden.

Love is a struggle between our longing to fuse ourselves with another and our fear that in the process we may lose our own identity and freedom. If we do not understand the nature of this conflict, we may interpret normal feelings of hesitation as evidence that we are not really in love. Oddly enough, hesitation can often mean the opposite — that we are passing from a phase of infatuation and idealization to one in which we may begin to love a real person.

Understanding our own hesitations may be hard, but realizing that the one we love also has doubts can be devastating. In Emma Turpin's painting a wary lover is approaching a seemingly uninterested woman. The scene is overlooked by a distant, Cupid-like figure.

This transition is hard for narcissistic people — those who have transferred their self-love to an ideal Other and resent any faults or weaknesses in the image they have created. The heavy demands that we make on the person we want to love are among the greatest obstacles to making a lasting commitment. The strong and the proud also find it difficult to accept the vulnerability inherent in a full commitment to another person. They may feel they are showing weakness by admitting that they need someone.

Shows of indifference, hesitation, reluctance or outright hostility are, of course, also part of the age-old game of love. Women were once expected to pretend to spurn men's advances — and were valued all the more if they did. Games of resistance were often ritualized: in Andalusia, three formal refusals before acceptance were once the rule of correct courtship.

However, feelings of ambivalence are more than just a ruse. Most of us feel alternating desire and resistance — and even experience moods of alternating love and hate. The Irish poet Thomas Moore described the fascination of these violently fluctuating emotions: "When I loved you, I can't but allow / I had many an exquisite minute / But the scorn that I feel for you now / Hath even more luxury in it!" Hatred can, in fact, sometimes be a deep-rooted psychological defence against making the ultimate commitment of loving someone.

Dream relationships in which couples never quarrel and continue to see each other as perfect in every respect are rare. For many of us, the key moment in any love affair is when we begin to notice physical or personality blemishes, or when differences of opinion and other irritants of everyday life begin to intrude into the relationship. If we survive this first serious analysis and can find each other's human weaknesses touching, the relationship is probably moving into a more stable phase.

Modern sexual freedom means that we are likely to reach this key moment sooner than lovers did in the past, as the process of courtship is less prolonged and artificial. We know each other better sooner and can be as honest as we want without having to manufacture the correct emotion for the sake of a social code. However, the commitment of saying "I love you" and meaning it is no less serious than it was, and hesitation before saying it is not necessarily a sign that our love is half-hearted.

Nelly Erichsen's The Orchard *is a symbolically charged setting for a lover's attempt to overcome the uncertainties shown by his hesitant sweetheart.*

THE BUNGLER

You glow in my heart
Like the flames of uncounted candles.
But when I go to warm my hands,
My clumsiness overturns the light,
And then I stumble
Against the tables and chairs.

Amy Lowell (1874–1925)

NEED AND PROTECTION

"My love is selfish. I cannot breathe without you," Keats wrote to Fanny Brawne. His letters reveal the agony of a man who believes that his great love is not greatly returned and who needs to be loved with an equal passion and equally undivided attention.

Need seems to be part of all human love, however much some of us are reluctant to admit it. According to Plato, Socrates used this argument to rebut the idea that Eros was a god. Eros, he said, was the son of Poverty and therefore was always in need, always yearning for something. How can a god be needful?

The Christian philosopher C. S. Lewis described God's love for humanity as "gift love". Protective human love — parental love, for example — is also a form of unconditional "gift love" which is seldom repeated in adult relationships. However, lovers may assume parent-child roles, one partner predominantly protecting and giving, the other constantly needing and receiving love.

Jan van Eyck's The Arnolfini Marriage *is filled with symbols of the married state. The dog signifies fidelity and the candle represents the eye of God.*

Before our own time, the idea that men were protectors and women were in need of protection was one of the most deeply ingrained of all cultural traditions. Monsters threatened women, only to be slain by suitably heroic men. Romantic Hollywood films of the 1940s showed men releasing women from monsters of the mind — neurotic illness caused by domestic tyranny, such as Elizabeth Barrett's cruel father. "Thy soul hath snatched up mine, all faint and weak / And placed it by thee on a golden throne," she wrote to her husband Robert, after marriage had released her from her father's regime.

The concept of a strong, protective male supporting the delicate and vulnerable female was a powerful 19th-century archetype. It reflected women's weaker social and economic position, as well as a Western ideal of feminine sensitivity and fragility. However, the succouring, healing aspects of love were also associated with the female role, and could paradoxically place the woman in the emotionally stronger position. In medieval romances, the lady is often her knight's protector as well as his inspiration, binding his literal or figurative wounds

In his painting The Lovers, *Picasso portrays a young man supporting his lover in a tender and protective embrace. The sense of security evoked by a partner's presence is a valuable corrective to the pressures of modern lifestyles.*

and offering the gentle solace of love. Modern writings on love are very aware of the dynamics of power in a relationship: the relative strength of each partner is fluid, dependent upon individuals and changing circumstances, and not determined solely by gender.

Need-love is not necessarily selfish, but it can become stifling if it turns into an addiction. Some lovers become so emotionally demanding that they are impossible to satisfy. In the best kind of love, both partners need and protect, give and receive — and admit to doing so.

UNREQUITED LOVE

The more powerfully we are attracted to someone we meet, the harder it is to believe that the electricity that we feel crackling between us may not be a reciprocal current, but simply the reflected energy of our own emotion. To discover this later on in a relationship can be even more confusing.

If it is any comfort, this painful realization is one that nearly everyone makes at some time in their lives. According to Ovid's myth of the beautiful youth Adonis, the goddess of love herself was similarly humiliated when Adonis impatiently rejected her advances, and longed only to go hunting. In Shakespeare's poem "Venus and Adonis", Cupid's arrow is powerless to affect him. Venus, bewildered and frustrated, accuses Adonis of an obsessive self-love: "Narcissus so himself forsook / And died to kiss his shadow in the brook."

In this 15th-century tapestry a courtly lover surrenders his heart to his lady, seated in a sensual garden of love.

Psychologists tell us that narcissism is indeed one of the reasons why some people are unable to respond to love. They may wish to be treated as their ideal self. Or they may have formulated an imaginary, idealized Other, so specific that the chance of such a threatening encounter is fairly remote. However, this is an extreme case. We are much more likely to suffer unrequited love simply because we have made the mistake of assuming that our own feelings are experienced by another. There is really no reason to expect another person to reciprocate our love — unless we overlook the fact that passion is not a rational or logical experience. Love can strike us with such force that we tend to forget how singular it is. It may distort our perception, allowing us to make fools of ourselves as a result. A famous example is the sour steward Malvolio in Shakespeare's *Twelfth Night*, who absurdly believes himself loved by the lady whom he serves. Yet he has nothing on which to base this supposition but a cryptic letter, designed to tease him.

Arab poets in the 9th century praised those who deliberately and bravely accepted the poignancy and anguish of unrequited love. Their conception of true love entailed dedication to an idealized Beloved, whose favours were never sought. This might be because she was unattainable or because the lover preferred not to tarnish his elevated emotion by carnal desire. The Prophet Muhammad was believed to have said: "He who loves and remains chaste, never reveals his secret, and dies, dies a martyr's death." This notion influenced the Italian poet Dante, who did not seek to consummate an idealized love for his inspiration, Beatrice. She remained an unattainable symbol of the Supreme Beloved, shining with divine radiance.

Some people deliberately choose to love someone inaccessible because it avoids all possibility of being rejected or disappointed. A truer – and more agonizing – form of unrequited love involves a refusal to accept rejection. The emotional charge is sustained by a desperate hope that this love will one day be returned, together with an inconsolable longing. The Greeks named this longing after a special god, Antieros, brother of Eros. It can be a creative impetus and has produced some of the world's most poignant poetry – notably the many love poems W. B. Yeats wrote to the Irish beauty Maude Gonne, who was to marry another man.

Edward Hopper's City Sunlight *may strike a chord in those who have waited up all night only to realize, in the cold light of day, that their lover is not going to call.*

LOVE AND JEALOUSY

One of the greatest challenges in love is to contend with the range of darker emotions it may unleash in us. Jealousy is one of the most frequently encountered, a feeling which we almost universally disdain but which is so integral to our experience of passion that it has been described as love's shadow. "Nobody can love who is not jealous," claimed André le Chapelain in his celebrated *Rules of Love* in the 13th century, in unexpected affirmation of what we perceive as a mean-spirited and destructive emotion. On a grand scale, epitomized by Shakespeare's tragic hero Othello, it is far blinder than love could ever be.

Intense jealousy is often also the first sign that we are in love. If we have missed or undervalued all the other signals, the appearance of a rival concentrates the mind wonderfully. As its Greek origin in the word *zelos* suggests, jealousy implies an intense, ardent interest in something. Passion feeds on jealousy, and some know precisely how to exploit their lover's suspicions or insecurities. In this gambit of love, desire is artificially sustained by a threat, and it is true that people sometimes fully value a love only when they are jealous. Emotional security can, paradoxically, be almost stifling.

Psychologists have identified three types of jealousy – delusional, projected and competitive. Delusional jealousy, peculiarly dangerous and cruelly unfair, is the form dramatized in *Othello*, where the villainous Iago plants and nourishes Othello's insecurity. Irrational jealousy can create its own certainties, as Iago is well aware: "Trifles light as air are to the jealous / Confirmations strong as proofs of holy writ." Using no more than a stolen handkerchief and a few misconstrued conversations, he cynically manipulates Othello into believing that Desdemona has been unfaithful – and murdering her.

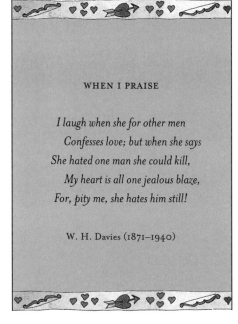

WHEN I PRAISE

I laugh when she for other men
Confesses love; but when she says
She hated one man she could kill,
My heart is all one jealous blaze,
For, pity me, she hates him still!

W. H. Davies (1871–1940)

In Frans Masereel's early 20th-century woodcut, a woman arranges a rendezvous with her lover under the eyes of her older husband.

Above left: This painting by Ingres depicts an encounter of the lovers Francesca da Rimini and Paolo, her husband's brother. The adulterous couple were executed by her husband in 1389.

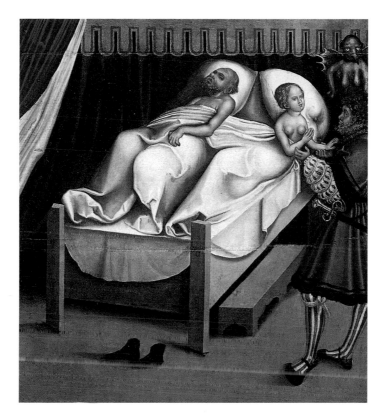

Projected jealousy is less malignant, but it may also destroy love if we let it. This type of jealousy perceives harmless flirtations or friendships to be in themselves disloyalties. An intensely possessive love may make us fear anybody that distracts our lover's attention. We can be driven to try to restrict the other's freedom or to spy on any part of their life that lies outside our control.

Competitive jealousy, by contrast, is often completely justified. A real betrayal is one of the most acutely painful experiences in love, and well merits a strong reaction. Less easy to negotiate is the antagonism provoked by straightforward rivalry for another's love. One problem is that distorted perception may overestimate a rival's success. A lighter approach is usually better than a furious outburst — be it of passion or temper — which may reflect unfavourably on the "wronged" lover. A common form of retaliation is the teasing attempt to inspire reciprocal jealousy in the beloved — often a successful tactic, as long as the game-playing does not become out of control.

In Cranach's painting from the early 16th century, a beautiful woman slips out of bed into the arms of her lover. Her husband continues to sleep, while a medieval devil views the scene with approval.

LOVE TRIANGLES

Duels offered a traditional way for gentlemen to dispose of their rivals in love. The custom was only outlawed in the 19th century.

One of the most frequent reasons for lack of happiness in love is the existence of a triangle of some sort. A rival is often involved at either the beginning or the end of a relationship, leading to a three-way situation in which at least one person feels anguished — and sometimes all three.

A fundamental tenet of traditional romantic love is that it is fixed upon a single other soul. Yet romantic literature is often dominated by triangular relationships. Courtly love, because it was mainly adulterous, itself involved a triangle, as in the story of the legendary King Arthur, his queen Guinevere and his trusted friend Sir Lancelot. The ardour of the knight and his lady was intensified by the alternating joy and despair of having and not having, winning and losing in the complex interplay of a triangular, clandestine relationship.

Yet some who find themselves in a triangle discover that their experience of love is sharpened and even enhanced by it. The exquisite pain of being unsure that they are loved completely is, for certain lovers, the essence of passion. They may need the spur of jealousy to believe fully that they are in love. For others, deliberately maintaining a love triangle offers a dangerous sense of excitement — and perhaps an unacknowledged sense of emotional security. Such a situation enables lovers to avoid the risks inherent in making any final commitment to a singular love — which may threaten their valued personal freedom. Instead, the impermanence creates its own security, and they are able to maintain two lovers in a tantalizing state of indecision — at least for a while.

The Merciless Lady, *a painting by the Pre-Raphaelite*
artist Dante Gabriel Rossetti, shows a girl looking on helplessly
as her lover becomes fascinated by another.

*D*rink to me only with thine eyes,
    And I will pledge with mine;
Or leave a kiss but in the cup,
    And I'll not look for wine.
The thirst that from the soul doth rise,
    Doth ask a drink divine:
But might I of Jove's nectar sup,
    I would not change for thine.

I sent thee late a rosy wreath,
    Not so much honouring thee,
As giving it a hope, that there
    It could not withered be.
But thou thereon did'st only breathe,
    And sent'st it back to me;
Since when it grows and smells, I swear,
    Not of itself, but thee.

Ben Jonson (1572–1637), "Song: To Celia"

When I lie prone above your lovely face
Your eyes reveal strange glints of white, of black,
And my whole bloodstream seethes along its track
Right to the heart itself the colours race.
What they disclose is Love, who changes place,
Now low, now high, bow bent and staring back.
Shot after shot I suffer his attack.
Reason, if I'm deluded, state your case!

Such loss of self-control these visions bring
I would betray my father and my king,
My sisters, brothers, mother — yes, and France.
So crazed I am, having drunk long and well
A venom spurted by our dalliance
Out of the eyes which hold me in their spell.

Pierre de Ronsard (1524–85), "Meslanges, 2, VI",

trs from the French by Laurence Kitchin

LOVE AND MADNESS

In this illustration from The Book of Good Morals, *the two characters' alter egos are trying to persuade them to act irrationally, against their better judgment.*

"To live and to suffer — heaven, hell — that is what I want to feel," wrote Julie de Lespinasse, mistress of the 18th-century French philosopher and mathematician Jean d'Alembert. Her ardent love letters expressed the desire, shared by many romantic lovers, to "love as one must love: excessively, to the point of madness and despair".

The concept of love as an all-consuming passion, an obsession sweeping away reason or conventions, was a grand theme of 19th-century romantic novels and operas. However, it has a much older history than that. The extremes of love have always been seen as a divine madness. Countless portraits of women as sphinx-like creatures concealing smouldering passions betray men's fears of arousing a venomous or insatiable lover. From literature to Hollywood movies, a series of vengeful harpies embody the male fear that love may, literally, drive women crazy.

In reality, it may frequently be the sanest, most rational thinkers of both sexes who become unhinged by an obsessive love, often for a wildly unsuitable object. The English essayist William Hazlitt, for example, recorded his entirely absurd, passionate feelings of jealousy over his landlady's daughter, only half his own age.

Psychologists describe this type of love as a form of complete selfishness. Elevated to the status of a god, love demands an obedience so complete that we become deaf to our own conscience. Mad, passionate love excuses much, but we are still troubled if it is used to justify aban- doning everything else.

There is a disturbing
undercurrent of violence
in this late 18th–century
painting of a courtier
and his lover.

LOVE AND LAUGHTER

The bacchanalian fever that swept through Europe at the end of the 19th century led to many extraordinary romances.

This 18th-century needlework panel, entitled Spring, celebrates the carefree joys of youthful love.

Cruel though laughter can seem to a lover whose heart is breaking, humour is an essential ingredient in successful relationships — sometimes the key one. If it can be endured, self-mockery is an invaluable corrective to the miseries of obsessive love.

Much of Greek mythology consists of a vast, sprawling comedy of amorous escapades. The Arabic concept of love as a serious art form, with its own elaborate rituals and courtesies, may itself have been paradoxically based on humour. The 20th-century historian Theodore Zeldin has suggested that the surprising Bedouin tolerance of joking familiarities between women and visiting strangers first helped to break down restrictive convention. This in turn facilitated many later adventures of passionate love. He quotes a Bedouin song that asks, "What between us two brought love, in the valley of Bagid?" and answers that it was the joking insults that the couple exchanged. "Of love, the first part is jesting and the last part right earnestness," wrote the influential 11th-century Moorish theologian, Ibn Hazm.

Erotic love, especially if it involves breaking rules and the consequent risks of exposure, is always poised on the edge of farce. Its more absurd aspects are depicted by Geoffrey Chaucer in the *Miller's Tale*, one of the earliest and bawdiest love stories in the English language — and the first of a thousand bedroom farces. However, the master of love and comedy is Shakespeare, for whom courtship is essentially a matter of wit and mirth. Even the youthful, tragic and idealistic Juliet is able to laugh at herself. Humour is seen as one of the greatest female weapons of courtship: among Shakespeare's most attractive and verbally agile heroines are Beatrice in *Much Ado About Nothing* and Viola in *Twelfth Night*. In *As You Like It*, the charming Rosalind skilfully trades jests with the court fool, and warns her own love, Orlando: "Make the doors fast upon a woman's wit, and it will out at the casement; shut that and 'twill out at the keyhole; stop that, 'twill fly with the smoke out at the chimney."

Comedy has always been love's safety valve, which explains the often unexpected romantic success of those who have the ability to make others giggle. The tensions and uncertainties of first love can be eased by laughter. Teasing is an essential way in which we test the strength of a new relationship as well as a way of holding someone at arms' length until we are more confident that we know what our feelings for one another are. Few things are as binding as shared laughter, nor is there anything so divisive as finding that the person we think we love has a different sense of humour — or worse still, none at all. Humour has to be part of any lasting relationship, if only as a device to end the kind of quarrel in which both have taken up positions that can only be defused by a shared joke.

Masked balls often became more riotous than normal dances, as guests' inhibitions were released by their facial disguises. The events offered a tantalizing juxtaposition of secret intimacy within a very public sphere.

Wit and humour run through love poetry and songs with the same leavening effect. They may take the form of outrageous comparisons or of the acute, ironic insights born of experience. The tone adopted in comic descriptions of love is as diverse as the situations themselves, ranging from the mocking cuteness of Henry S. Lee's: "My love she is a kitten / And my heart's a ball of string" to the wry observations of Dorothy Parker: "By the time you say you're his / Shivering and sighing; / And he vows his passion is / Infinite, undying / Lady make a note of this / One of you is lying." No matter what the pain of love is, it seems that some can see its humorous aspects and find comfort in the healing power of laughter.

LASTING LOVE

This Greek funeral relief depicts a married couple who hoped to remain united after death.

"Happily ever after" is usually where the story ends in all the fairytales of love. Lasting love is not the stuff of romantic fiction because the edge of pursuit, drama, danger, uncertainty and, we assume, wild physical passion, has gone. What interests readers is unhappy love. Paradoxically, lasting love sounds almost dull by comparison — and yet it is what every lover seeks. For who can really endure the thought of their love affair ending?

Perhaps tradition has implanted in our hearts the idea that love is ephemeral. In medieval stories of courtly love, most romances ended on a tragic note. It was believed that if every obstacle to love were removed and the lovers actually married each other, their passion would soon dwindle and disappear. Our own century may be the first in which there has been a generally accepted belief that marriage is compatible with romantic love — and this remains predominantly a Western idea.

A few great writers have always stood out against the prevailing cynicism. One of Shakespeare's greatest sonnets celebrates a deeper conception of love: "Love's not Time's fool, though rosy lips and cheeks / Within his bending sickle's compass come / Love alters not with his brief hours and weeks / But bears it out even to the edge of doom." In a lasting relationship, we may no longer be sick with desire every time we set eyes on the person we love, but this does not mean that many happily married people do not yearn for each other when parted, or continue to find each other sexually exciting. Still less does it mean that sentiment fades with the initial exuberant sensuality.

Pierre Choderlos de Laclos, the 18th-century French author of *Les Liaisons dangereuses*, one of the most cynical books ever penned about love, also wrote a surprisingly tender prescription for a

Vincent van Gogh's The Siesta *portrays an established couple resting quietly together after a hard morning's labour.*

MEN SAY THE PASSIONS SHOULD GROW OLD

*Men say the passions should grow old
With passing years; my heart
Is incorruptible as gold,
'Tis my immortal part.
Nor is there any god can lay
On love the finger of decay.*

"Michael Field", the pen name of Katherine Bradley (1846–1914) and Edith Cooper (1862–1914)

happy marriage: "Each studies the other, observes himself or herself closely in the other's presence, finds out what tastes and personal preferences will have to be given up for the common peace." He believes that this will soon create "that gentle friendship, that tender confidence which, added to respect, seems to me to be the true, the solid happiness of marriage. The illusions of love may be sweeter, but who does not know that they are less enduring?" The experiences of many lovers confirm this as one of love's fundamental truths — possibly the most surprising one of all.

The golden ecstasy that is experienced early on in a relationship is portrayed in Gustav Klimt's The Kiss. Its memory may act as a bond even after initial passion has faded.

Books offering advice on how to sustain erotic love have been popular for many centuries. This illustration forms part of a manuscript from the early 15th century.

The ideals advocated by a modern psychologist might differ very little from de Laclos's suggestions: sexual equality, compatible interests, freedom from envy, mutual respect, acceptance of separate identities. Qualities such as these, together with the tenderness of a couple who have loved each other with real passion, and not forgotten it, provide the true ingredients of lasting love. The challenge and adventure of love do not end when lovers marry. That is where the real test of love often begins.

75

LOST LOVE

Lost love, remembered and regretted, is the greatest theme not only of lyrical poetry, but also of opera and popular music. Nobody has expressed it more simply than the Chilean poet Pablo Neruda: "Tonight I can write the saddest lines. / To think that I do not have her. To feel that I have lost her. / To hear the immense night, still more immense without her."

As soon as we fall in love we become vulnerable to — and peculiarly defenceless against — its loss. This is one of the risks that we take for love: that the person in whom we have invested so many of our hopes and dreams, and so much longing, may go away, or fall out of love with us, or leave us for someone else, or be separated from us by some malign fate, or be mistakenly left by us — or even die.

Puccini's opera *La Bohème*, the most heart-rending of romantic operas, dramatizes the fears of all lovers — that passionate love cannot last and that we may suffer the agony of watching the beloved die before our eyes. The essence of romantic opera is happiness under threat: fragile, ephemeral, doomed.

In a sense, all lost love is a kind of death. What we feel is a grief as real as any caused by actual death, often sharpened to an unendurable pitch by the fact that all of our senses are involved — our whole being is missing the warmth, closeness and intimate delight of another loved body. Losing our love to another is acutely painful, and can lead to lingering bitterness if we let it. Yet if we can overcome such possessiveness, the experience of losing in love may also mature us — and be a preparation for something more lasting.

In loving we make ourselves vulnerable to enormous hurt. The loneliness and despair that we feel on losing a loved one, vividly evoked in this painting by Emma Turpin, has been compared to the numbing shock of a bereavement.

Ariadne helped Theseus to defeat the Minotaur, only to be abandoned by him on the island of Naxos. She later married the god Dionysus (see page 27) and found true happiness. During the Renaissance she became a symbol of the restoration of life through death.

In the dusky path of a dream I went to seek the love who
was mine in a former life.

Her house stood at the end of a desolate street.
In the evening breeze her pet peacock sat drowsing on its
perch, and the pigeons were silent in their corner.

She set her lamp down by the portal and stood before me.
She raised her large eyes to my face and mutely asked, "Are
you well my friend?"
I tried to answer, but our language had been lost and
forgotten.

I thought and thought; our names would not come to
my mind.
Tears shone in her eyes. She held up her right hand to
me. I took it and stood silent.

One lamp had flickered in the evening breeze and died.

Rabindranath Tagore (1861–1941), "In the Dusky Path of a Dream",
trs from the Bengali by the author

*S*hall I compare thee to a summer's day?

Thou art more lovely and more temperate:

Rough winds do shake the darling buds of May,

And summer's lease hath all too short a date:

Sometime too hot the eye of heaven shines,

And often is his gold complexion dimmed;

And every fair from fair sometime declines,

By chance, or nature's changing course, untrimmed;

But thy eternal summer shall not fade,

Nor lose possession of that fair thou owest,

Nor shall death brag thou wander'st in his shade,

When in eternal lines to time thou growest;

    So long as men can breathe, or eyes can see,

    So long lives this, and this gives life to thee.

William Shakespeare (1564–1616), Sonnet 18

THE LANGUAGE OF LOVE

Love hath a language of his own
A voice that goes
From heart to heart — whose mystic tone
Love only knows.

ANON, PERSIAN LOVE POEM

The language of love is largely private and unspoken. A lingering look, a touch, the answering pressure of a hand, can speak more directly and thrillingly than words could ever do. Most people are not poets, and ordinary language can appear desperately short of the emotional intensity that lovers feel. We find ourselves uttering near banalities, falling back on words that seem drained of the very meaning that we want them to convey.

This is perhaps why lovers have for centuries found other ways to communicate — more individual, more personal, and often mysterious to anyone else. Only lovers really understand the emotional charge that lies behind a book or piece of music sent from one to the other, a memento, keepsake, ring, or flower — or the pet names used when they are together.

THE LOOK OF LOVE

Helen of Troy, the most beautiful woman in the world, is shown here gazing at her husband Menelaus.

The eyes are the most immediate and powerful communicators of our emotions. It is almost impossible to mistake the feelings that they convey. Medieval writers believed that the process of falling in love began with the meeting of eyes, which they called the windows of the soul. They thought that a mystical transfusion found its way to the heart, producing the sensation of love by an almost alchemical reaction.

We learn to appreciate and respond to the look of love almost from the time that we are born. Babies will search their mother's face until they focus on her eyes — and then smile, reassured by the glow of love they find there. Lovers almost get lost in each other's gaze, oblivious to the smiles of the outside world. The eyes express love both consciously and unconsciously: dilated pupils, for example, are a classic signal of sexual arousal and eye make-up continues to be a major weapon in the battery of allure.

Spanish women, the inheritors of Moorish veils, were said to be able to play more games with their eyes than conjurors could with a pack of cards. In their ever-shifting language of flirtation, men might take a sideways movement of the eyes as a question, a blank stare as suffering, a wink as joy, an inward look as refusal, touched eyelids as a warning and lowered lids as consent. The most thrilling look was the sidelong "flash of lightning". However, the look of love has no guarantee — an essential part of its charm. Everything can be said with the eyes, but nothing can be proven, as Stendhal was to observe: "Glances are the big guns of the virtuous coquette; everything can be conveyed in a look, and yet that look can always be denied."

*This painting by Emma Turpin conveys the powerful attraction
that can be aroused by even a casual glance.*

PUBLIC AND PRIVATE

"They love indeed who quake to say they love," wrote the most famous soldier-poet of the 16th century, Sir Philip Sidney. Declaring love for the first time, when so many of our hopes rest on the response, has never been easy. Even if we believe that our love is returned, we may not immediately want to share our secret with the world.

The urge to shout love from the rooftops conflicts with a feeling that making it public in some way diminishes its mystic intensity. Do we really welcome the witty

18th-century Venice was famous for its ridottos, or masked dancing parties. This detail from a painting by Pietro Longhi shows a pair of lovers flirting in the safety of their disguise.

observations made by even our closest friends? This instinctive reticence was almost a rule of love in some earlier societies. Courtly love was usually secretive, and André le Chapelain's 13th-century *Rules of Love* advised that "a love divulged seldom lasts." This reflected the codes of a time when the penalties for unsanctioned love were very high, and disclosure could bring down hostility, opposition, shame or complete social ruin on those involved.

We are far less secretive now — and may seem to have less reason to hide our love. In the 19th century, romantic love was essentially a private matter and public signs of affection were thought distasteful; even in the 1940s, lovers kissing or embracing in public were an almost exotic sight outside Paris. Yet the change may be more superficial than it first seems. Love still moves as it has always done between private and public worlds, testing the limits of each. The contrast can be piquant, as anyone knows who has held hands under the table at a formal dinner. Lovers still walk into the ordinary world carrying the secrets of their own extraordinary and sensual intimacy. However, the wider world has continued to provide the moral and social context into which love must fit if it is not to remain completely selfish — and in the end become claustrophobic.

The trouble is that, cut off completely from the public world, it is too easy for any kind of love to seem wonderful. This is one of the reasons why so many holiday

romances happen. They seem to offer, at least for a while, love without any of its usual consequences. We do not have to measure our lover's suitability against the potentially conflicting demands of family, friends, children, careers, money or security.

    Moving from a private love affair to a public one has always been seen as a serious step, which takes a certain amount of courage and shows commitment. It signifies that we trust those whom we admire to approve of our choice, and recognize that they should not be excluded from our happiness. In effect, we are acknowledging that we do not inhabit a totally private world of timeless ecstasy — or even a small world of like-minded friends — and that the language of real love is public as well as private.

In Willy Ronis's photo-graph Café rue de la Hachette, *an attentive man lights a woman's cigarette. The power of the image lies in the tension between this intimate gesture and the very public surroundings.*

THE MUSIC OF LOVE

Traditionally, love songs were performed by men in Europe and the Middle East. This late 18th-century painting depicts a young Persian musician.

Love songs have for centuries provided a language of love far more eloquent and flexible than most of us who try to express our feelings. They can touch and move us in a way that cuts completely across the usual boundaries of age, social milieu or aesthetic taste — as even the ultra-sophisticated Noël Coward noted when he wrote in *Private Lives*: "Strange how potent cheap music is."

The power of music, and its ability to celebrate love, dominates the ancient Greek myth of Orpheus. Following the death of his adored wife Eurydice, the musician-poet descends into the depths of the Underworld to rescue her, enchanting the cold heart of Hades, the God of the Dead, with the songs of his enduring love. The link between music and love songs has continued through history. In the musical salons of 7th-century Medina, beautiful, long-haired youths are believed to have played lutes and sung the praises of love as the very essence of life. In the 11th century the troubadour poets brought the tradition of courtly love to Europe, and music became seen as an essential ingredient of a secular love celebrated as the origin of virtue. These travelling musicians, often illiterate, were the predecessors of this century's great writers of love songs, from Cole Porter to Stephen Sondheim.

Love songs are more, however, than Sigmund Romberg's tender definition: "just a caress set to music". Folk ballads, country music, torch songs or rock songs all tell stories about lovers whose emotions we can identify with and which, in a sense, become our own while the song endures. The lyrics of love songs, from operatic arias or Schubert's delicate *Lieder* to the ultimate simplicity of the Beatles' "Love, love me do!", create infinite variations on a theme that we might have thought was finite.

88

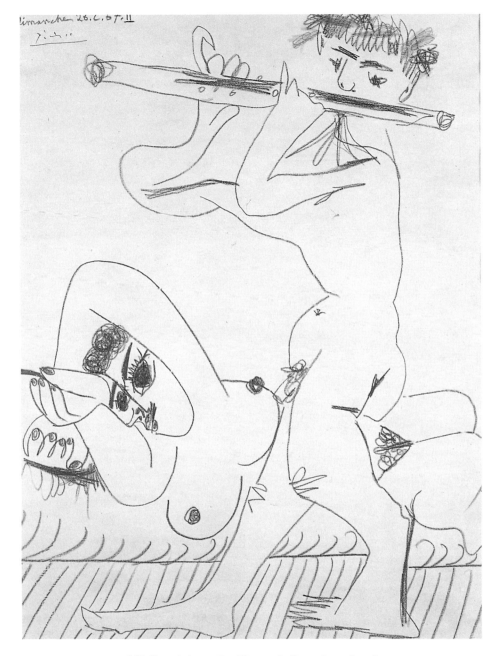

Pablo Picasso's drawing Pan Playing the Pipes *depicts the god
seducing a woman with his wild music. Pan was an ancient fertility
deity, and the inspiration for pastoral poetry.*

THE DANCE OF LOVE

This wondrous myracle did Love devise
For Daancing is Love's proper exercise.

SIR JOHN DAVIES (1569–1626), "ORCHESTRA: A POEM OF DAUNCING"

Dance is courtship in full flight. Its permitted embrace has been for centuries the most openly erotic of society's flirtation rituals, and was consequently often attacked by the moral guardians of society. The 17th-century pamphleteer William Prynne, for example, condemned dancing for being for "the most part attended with many amorous smiles, wanton compliments, unchaste kisses … lust-provoking attire, ridiculous love pranks, all of which savour only of sensuality, of raging fleshly lusts." Many formal dances, such as the quadrille and others popular in 19th-century English assembly rooms, allowed little physical contact between the partners. Emotion could be conveyed only by shared, sidelong glances, lowered eyes and murmured conversation, for the dance floor was one of the few occasions where chaperoned young ladies might speak to men directly and alone.

The most criticized dance of all was the waltz, in which couples circled the floor together, clasped in a close embrace. The dance swept across Europe in the early 1800s and soon crossed the Atlantic, prompting a flood of sermons and articles, as well as a tongue-in-cheek poem by Byron about its voluptuous seductions. Yet dancing never stopped, perhaps because no one, not even those alarmed by the latest style, can forget their own dancing days — celebrated even by the cynical Byron: "On with the dance! let joy be unconfined / No sleep till morn, when youth and pleasure meet / To chase the glowing hours with flying feet."

Every society through history has used the sensual power of dance, whether to delight the gods or simply the other sex. In the Bible, for example, the sexual charge of Salome's dance for King Herod secured her the head of John the Baptist as a reward. Bizet's tempestuous heroine Carmen exploits the tantalizing art of gypsy flamenco to ensnare her

At balls women were provided with dance cards on which to record their partners' names. These were prized as souvenirs long after the event itself. Ladies were encouraged to select several partners; to dance with the same man more than twice was to risk censure.

90

In Europe during the 18th and 19th centuries dancing was one of the few activities that allowed close contact between men and women. The waltz, which allowed men to clasp their partners' waists, caused outrage when it was first introduced, but it became wildly popular.

lovers José and Escamillo the bullfighter. Latin-American dances, such as the tango and samba, contain a powerful erotic charge, and in the 1920s flamboyant performances of the popular Charleston became the hallmark of the emancipated "flapper".

Dancing has not lost its power in courtship. Prom dances in America and débutante balls in Europe are events as momentous — and as keenly anticipated — as great aristocratic balls were in the 18th century. The rituals of amorous smiles, whispered compliments and suggestive movements continue to link dancing with courtship and love.

THE FOODS OF LOVE

This sumptuous painting depicts an actual banquet held at the Ca Rezzonico, Venice, in September 1755. Such occasions of great festivity were enlivened by exotic foods and flirtation.

The imagery of love and food is deeply intermingled, as both the anticipation and the actual experience of each carries a powerful sensual charge. Sexual love and desire are often described as an unquenchable physical thirst or appetite, which may remain tantalizingly unfulfilled or be indulged to excess.

The thoughtful preparation of a meal for a loved one is consequently filled with great romantic significance. The hero of Ben Jonson's play *Volpone* promises to create for his love a meal of extraordinary rarity: "The heads of parrots, tongues of nightingales / The brains of peacocks and ostriches / Shall be our food: and could we get the phoenix, / Though nature lost her kind, she were our dish."

Love-potions, magical birds and the reputedly great aphrodisiac powers of raw oysters may or may not serve to augment love. Yet the real intimacy of shared food is both the perfect prelude to lovers' encounters and a powerful part in our nostalgic memories of them. Edwin Morgan's "Strawberries" recalls such an occasion with mouth-watering intensity: "the blue plates in our laps / the strawberries glistening / in the hot sunlight / we dipped them in sugar / looking at each other / not hurrying the feast / for one to come ..." The strawberry, an ancient symbol of carnal pleasure, is only one of a dozen fruits linked for centuries with the drama of erotic surrender.

European colonization of Africa, Asia and the Americas resulted in the import of many strange foods. Several of these were believed to have aphrodisiac properties.

Come live with me and be my love,
And we will all the pleasures prove
That valleys, groves, hills, and fields,
Woods, or steepy mountain yields.

And we will sit upon the rocks,
Seeing the shepherds feed their flocks,
By shallow rivers to whose falls
Melodious birds sing madrigals.

And I will make thee beds of roses
And a thousand fragrant posies,
A cap of flowers, and a kirtle
Embroidered all with leaves of myrtle;

A gown made of the finest wool
Which from our pretty lambs we pull;
Fair lined slippers for the cold,
With buckles of the purest gold;

A belt of straw and ivy buds,
With coral clasps and amber studs:
And if these pleasures may thee move,
Come live with me, and be my love.

The shepherds' swains shall dance and sing
For thy delight each May morning:
If these delights thy mind may move,
Then live with me and be my love.

Christopher Marlowe (1564–93), "The Passionate Shepherd to His Love"

CODED LOVE

Lovers have always had secrets to keep, whether their love has been openly declared or not. Not saying exactly what you mean is part of the teasing fun of courtship, and has been an ingredient of flirtation for centuries. If you have not made up your mind about someone, or suspect that they may not have made up their mind about you, a degree of conversational evasiveness is essential.

Fans have been an instrument of flirtation for centuries. An adept coquette could show her annoyance, embarrassment, or willingness to listen to a lover by the way that she hid her gaze or fanned herself.

More serious codes have to be developed to communicate love in situations where its discovery would be at best embarrassing, at worst dangerous. Writing love letters in invisible ink or secret codes is a technique that goes back at least to Roman times. And throughout history, lovers have written coded messages to each other. Among the few to have survived are those of Lady Jane Whorwood, who smuggled letters to Royalist prisoners during the English Civil War. One particular letter promised a tryst in terms that must have been decoded with trembling hands: "Those cochineal-flecked breasts which you never before dared touch you may now graspe without asking my leave and kisse the sweetnesses thereof."

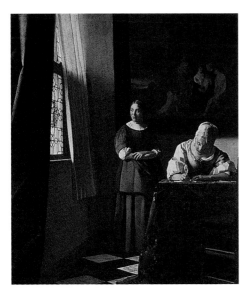

Women portrayed writing letters, such as this one painted by Vermeer, were traditionally assumed to be writing to a lover. Her trusted maidservant is waiting to deliver it.

Letters were the most common way to send illicit messages of love for centuries — and the most risky. They usually required a go-between — for example, a trusted maid or another servant. The intercepted letter leading to misunderstanding, shame, ruin, duels, suicide or murder has been the key plotting device in thousands of novels and plays. Lovers' codes seldom ran to more than simple ciphers with a prearranged key, but the young Mozart found a typically original way around his father's ban on writing to an admirer by sending messages to "my beautiful English rose" in which musical notes were substituted for letters of

THEY WHO ARE NEAR TO ME

*They who are near to me do not know that
you are nearer to me than they are.
They who speak to me do not know that my heart
is full with your unspoken words.
They who crowd in my path do not know that
I am walking alone with you.
They who love me do not know that their love
brings you to my heart.*

Rabindranath Tagore (1861–1941)

the alphabet. Another popular technique was the suggestive use of literary or mytho-logical allusions. The French queen Marie Antoinette left novels with passages underlined for her courtiers to find.

However, it was precisely the arts employed to conceal meaning from unwelcome eyes that enabled the writer's heart to speak directly to its true recipient — a paradox relished by generations of lovers and still thriving today.

Stanley Spencer's remarkable painting Love Letters
shows a man overwhelmed by the quantity — or perhaps
by the content — of the notes that he and
his lover are exchanging.

VALENTINES

The St Valentine's Day custom of lovers pledging themselves to each other is centuries old, though its association with two early Saints Valentine remains a mystery. A plausible origin of the tradition is suggested by Chaucer's 14th-century *Parlement of Foules*, which linked the saints' day on February 14 with the mating of birds — and, by extension, humans: "For this was on Seynt Valentynes day / When ev'ry fowl cometh to chese his make." The notion of a free-for-all selection of partners on February 14 may have grown out of this natural symbolism of early spring.

In the 16th and 17th centuries in England, a well-established tradition permitted women to select their valentines, by lot or by chance (for example, the first man sighted in the morning). A gift would then be expected from him in return. The celebrated diarist Samuel Pepys was clearly troubled by women having the upper hand in these matters, recording in an entry for 1662: "I did this day purposely shun to be seen at Sir W. Batten's — because I would not have his daughter to be my Valentine, there being no great friendship between us."

Highly elaborate letters and cards have been given and received by generations of lovers on St Valentine's Day.

This early 19th-century Swiss automaton snuff box would have been an extravagant token of love, although many Valentine gifts were less ornate.

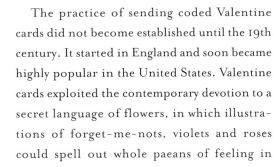

The practice of sending coded Valentine cards did not become established until the 19th century. It started in England and soon became highly popular in the United States. Valentine cards exploited the contemporary devotion to a secret language of flowers, in which illustrations of forget-me-nots, violets and roses could spell out whole paeans of feeling in complicated floral ciphers. Protected by anonymity, both men and women were able to take the initiative in declaring their love. "Never sign a valentine with your own name," was Sam Weller's advice to his master in Dickens' *Pickwick Papers*.

This mock $50 bill from the Bank of True Love was made in the USA in around 1850. It is an early example of the novelty card.

The endearments exchanged on our modern St Valentine's Day are just as elaborate and obscure. Newspapers are filled with cryptic messages from Squinky Pinky to Hunny Bunny, exciting Freudian analysts and delighting the rest of us with their tantalizing glimpses into the intimate, shared worlds of lovers. St Valentine's Day, this bizarre by product of the cult of two early Italian martyrs, preserves a thriving and remarkably ancient tradition. Six hundred years after Chaucer, the sexes still keep their annual appointment with each other, and mark the day with a variety of imaginative, entertaining and enduring rituals.

Floral messages on cards were charged with complex meanings. Lily of the valley and forget-me-nots, for example, symbolized a pure and steadfast love.

MESSAGES IN FLOWERS

The bright, warm colours of poppies have always held a particular charm for lovers.

Why is it no one ever sent me yet
One perfect limousine, do you
suppose?
Ah no, it's always just my luck to get
One perfect rose.

Dorothy Parker may have mocked the present of the single rose, but its power as an ambassador of love still transcends the cliché. Flowers have been emblems of secular and religious love for centuries. The very word "posy", for example, now meaning only a small bunch or nosegay, originally referred to a message of love, a piece of "poesy" (poetry), symbolized by the flowers themselves.

As gardens developed more widely in medieval Europe, flowers became charged with symbolic meanings. In Elizabethan England, the audiences at Shakespeare's *Hamlet* would have understood the resonances in Ophelia's speech to Laertes: "There is rosemary, that's for remembrance – pray you love, remember – and there is pansies, that's for thoughts."

However, it was not until the 19th century that these popular associations were formalized into an elaborate, secret language in which flowers were able to convey desires and sentiments that could not be openly expressed. Not surprisingly, the floral code did not remain a secret for long. Hundreds of books were published to help lovers decipher the illustrations on St Valentine's Day cards, or the meaning of a carefully crafted bouquet. More than just a parlour game, the code was based on the philosophical belief that truths could be expressed in natural forms. The language of flowers found its way into the fiction of Honoré de Balzac and Victor Hugo. In a novel, as in real life, floral symbolism could move the plot along without a word being spoken. For example, the gift of a white camellia – symbolizing loveliness – in Elizabeth Gaskell's novel *Ruth* would have been correctly interpreted by its readers as a bold, provocative move.

*Since ancient times the lotus has symbolized fertility, sexuality,
birth, rebirth and purity. In this Indian miniature the god Krishna
presents his beloved Radha with a lotus flower.*

TOKENS OF LOVE

Tokens of love, whether gained by accident or design, are a common theme in fairytales. This painting by Emma Turpin has resonances of Cinderella, in which Prince Charming finds the heroine again through her lost shoe.

Mark Antony may have pledged his kingdom for Cleopatra, but lovers have usually been content with smaller proofs of esteem. The long history of love's tokens and keepsakes reveals a bewildering range of objects, often trifling in themselves but all seeking to measure — and test — the power of love. Keepsakes are in some ways expressions of the doubts as much as the certainties that exist in human relationships. The value invested in a keepsake by the recipient is proof of regard for the giver — and such emotional significance may far exceed any material worth. Almost any small object might be pressed into service, from the purely pleasing (the solemnly worked pincushion of a 19th-century sailor) to the heavily symbolic, such as a lock of hair, implying a lover's surrender to the other. Early in his foreign travels, the young Lord Byron described how he had exchanged locks of hair with a "Spanish belle" at their parting. Regarding hers (about 3 feet in length) as something of an encumbrance, he sensibly sent it back to his mother in England.

Keepsakes were particularly popular when couples were parted by long absences, and objects in such cases were often chosen for their intimate connection with a person's body. A full list of the kinds of keepsakes a medieval woman might expect, in consolation for the travels of her roving knight, appeared in André le Chapelain's popular *Rules of Love* of the 13th century: "a handkerchief, a fillet for the hair, a wreath of gold or silver, a breastpin, a mirror or a girdle, a purse, a tassel, a comb, sleeves, gloves … any little gift useful for the care of the person, or pleasing to look at."

The keepsake could, of course, be a prelude to love, as well as confirmation of it.

Young lovers in Ancient Greece hung wreaths on their sweethearts' doors as a sign of affection.

The clasped hands on this gold bracelet from the early 19th century are an ancient symbol. Once representing a legal contract, it came to mean faith and love, and is a common feature on lovers' jewelry.

Spring, by Constantine Manos, *shows a man waiting to surprise his lover with a single rose — the most deeply romantic of all love tokens.*

In Shakespeare's *A Midsummer Night's Dream,* the spurned lover Egeus accuses his rival of having captured Hermia's heart by stealing "the impression of her fantasy / With bracelets of thy hair, rings, gawds, conceits, knacks, trifles, nosegays, sweetmeats ..." The desire to surprise a loved one with an unexpected present is a classic, never entirely altruistic, symptom of love. Perfumes, jewelry, books and items of clothing have been traditional favourites, as have gifts of music, from a single, poignant serenade to the latest, enduring CD. Even ephemeral items of food can play a significant role. Cleopatra, for example, was said to have ordered a wild boar to be roasted every hour in case her Antony should return.

The course of modern love is still punctuated with tokens and keepsakes, perhaps because the need to prove and reiterate love is stronger than ever. A particular present from a lover, or simply something he or she once wore, can be invested with almost talismanic properties. Nor should we forget that the photograph in a wallet or pocketbook is only the modern form of the miniature portraits that have been exchanged by lovers through the centuries.

Two hearts pierced by Cupid's arrow have become an international symbol of love. This lacquer box comes from Olimala in Mexico.

The heart shape has become synonymous with the word love, often replacing it on T-shirts and bumper stickers.

Is love a light for me? A steady light,
A lamp within whose pallid pool I dream
Over old love-books? Or is it a gleam,
A lantern coming towards me from afar
Down a dark mountain? Is my love a star?
Ah me! — so high above so coldly bright!

The fire dances. Is my love a fire
Leaping down the twilight muddy and bold?
Nay, I'd be frightened of him. I'm too cold
For quick and eager loving. There's a gold
Sheen on these flower petals as they fold
More truly mine, more like to my desire.

The flower petals fold. They are by the sun
Forgotten. In a shadowy wood they grow
Where the dark trees keep up a to-and-fro
Shadowy waving. Who will watch them shine
When I have dreamed my dream? Ah, darling mine,
Find them, gather them for me one by one.

Katherine Mansfield (1888–1923), "Secret Flowers"

*S*he walks in beauty, like the night

Of cloudless climes and starry skies;

And all that's best of dark and bright

Meet in her aspect and her eyes:

Thus mellowed to that tender light

Which heaven to gaudy day denies.

One shade the more, one ray the less,

Had half impaired the nameless grace

Which waves in every raven tress,

Or softly lightens o'er her face;

Where thoughts serenely sweet express

How pure, how dear their dwelling place.

And on that cheek, and o'er that brow,

So soft, so calm, yet eloquent,

The smiles that win, the tints that glow,

But tell of days in goodness spent,

A mind at peace with all below,

A heart whose love is innocent!

Lord Byron (1788–1824), "She Walks in Beauty"

COURTSHIP

A favourite diversion of the 18th-century aristocracy was to dress up as Arcadian shepherds and shepherdesses and conduct elegant flirtations.

The complicated and ever-shifting rules of Western courtship have always been based on the reasonable suspicion that when a man sets out to capture a woman's heart his primary motive is sex and not love. "Men prove much in vows but little in love," Viola tells Orsino in Shakespeare's *Twelfth Night*. Courtship is essentially a way of putting men's declarations of love to the test.

Courtship traditions go back to the 12th century, when the nobility of southern France, modelling themselves on Arabic and Moorish ideals, began to develop the arts of courtly love. This new romantic fashion was partly an elegant piece of theatre, a delightful pastime for bored wives and temporarily idle young men. Court ladies could practise their skills of flirtation without committing themselves to the risks of conducting an illicit affair, while their male "vassals" showed off their charm and wit. Notions of secular love as a gentle feminine tyranny, a test of men's virtue and a life-enhancing experience have permeated romantic literature ever since.

As courtship became seen as a prelude to marriage, rather than as an agreeable way of spending an afternoon, the process changed to one of establishing a man's social and economic suitability. In prosperous 19th-century society, courtship etiquette became extremely formal. Both the suitor and the father of his intended bride, for example, might be required to

This illuminated panel, from the Book of Hours of Charles of Angoulême, *illustrates the pleasures of spring. In medieval France courtship was a popular pastime with its own elaborate rules.*

wear black with white gloves during a meeting arranged to seek a woman's hand. However, parental permission gradually became less relevant, as Western couples began to select their own partners and marry for love.

The new rules of courtship that this required emerged most clearly in the United States, where the tests of love were increasingly conducted in private rather than in public. American love letters from the 19th century reveal repeated sequences of doubt, trial and reassurance as women tested men's professions of love by placing one obstacle after another in their path. This process of emotional assessment, foreshadowed in the novels of Jane Austen, established modern rules of courtship.

Dating rituals of the 1950s were not so different. Behind the pivotal high school prom with its meticulous hairdos and evening gowns, gleaming tuxedos and scrubbed faces, lay a similar if foreshortened process of tests and checks. Sexually, the barriers have gone down since then, and in the West dating and courting are now conducted far more informally. Yet where love is concerned, true bonding still requires a passage through some process of emotional trial and judgment. The difference in modern relationships — and it is a huge one — is that men and women increasingly test each other on an equal basis.

In Goya's The Parasol *a demure young woman is shielded from the sun by a servant. Her side-long glance and upheld fan suggest that she is an accomplished flirt.*

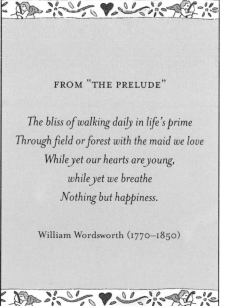

FROM "THE PRELUDE"

The bliss of walking daily in life's prime
Through field or forest with the maid we love
While yet our hearts are young,
while yet we breathe
Nothing but happiness.

William Wordsworth (1770–1850)

THE PROPOSAL

Among all love's rituals, the most awesome is the proposal of marriage. This instant is more powerfully charged than even the act of marriage itself, and its timing and setting assume an enduring significance. The proposal demands a daring leap of faith, since it cannot be tested in advance, any more than the first kiss can — nor can it be undone once spoken. Nowhere else in a relationship is one person so vulnerable to another, with all future hopes and plans depending on the outcome.

The proposal is primarily an emotional drama of the West, as Eastern conventions of arranged marriages rely on couples developing their love after the engagement, rather than before. Many Western traditions date from 19th-century proposals, in which nervous lovers, often relative strangers, inched across the gap between them. The agonizing uncertainty was reflected in broken sentences or clumsy avowals, such as the gloriously gruff declaration of love —

This illustration, from a 1921 fashion magazine, is entitled Oui! *It captures the moment at a dance when the two beautifully dressed lovers agree to marry.*

"Barkis is willin'" — in Charles Dickens' novel *David Copperfield*.

Of course, not all proposals succeed. Sometimes the stresses of the moment can prove overwhelming and the words remain unspoken. One of the most poignant scenes in literature occurs in *Anna Karenina*, when Kozynyshev, suddenly determined to propose to Varenka, despite his pledge of loyalty to a former, dead lover, approaches her in the woods. He knows from her flushed cheeks that she is expecting a proposal, "but instead of those words some perverse reflection caused him to ask: 'What is the difference between a white boletus and a birch mushroom?'" Each recognizes that the crucial moment has been irrevocably lost and cannot now ever be regained.

Modern proposals, often based on a much greater intimacy, still present lovers with an emotional challenge. Despite our supposed sophistication, the proposal remains a moment of exquisite awkwardness.

In this painting of a betrothal, a blindfolded Cupid prepares to fire
an arrow of love at the princess. Other suitors for her hand watch
apprehensively for her response.

111

THE RING

The ring is one of the most ancient forms of love-token. Originally used as the seal and emblem of authority, it is also a unique symbol of completeness, eternity and union. The early betrothal rings of the Romans, which were made of iron, were designed in the shape of two clasped hands to signify the exchange of legal vows. The first Christian wedding rings, which appeared around AD 860, are believed to have been worn originally on the fingers of the right hand, sometimes including the thumb. Only in the 16th century were they confined to the fourth finger of the left hand, for physiological reasons described in 1680 by Henry Swinburne: "by the received opinion of the learned ... in ripping up and anatomising men's bodies, there is a vein of blood, called *vena armoris*, which passeth from that finger to the heart." The left hand, as others said, was often also more practical.

In The Measure for the Wedding Ring, *a fiancé lovingly checks the size of his beloved's ring finger.*

The most common form of wedding ring — a plain gold band — dates back to Celtic times. Its classic simplicity has been increasingly favoured over showier versions, while the symbolic constancy of gold, whose properties survive the trials it may undergo, has become an established emblem of enduring love.

Engagement rings and other forms of love-jewelry have traditionally afforded more elaborate expressions of love, especially in Renaissance Europe, where rings contained bezels that hid tiny hearts or other romantic keepsakes. The 16th-century jemmel ring was composed of interlocking sections, which couples broke apart on betrothal and symbolically reassembled as a token of love on their wedding day. A century later, the elaborate decoration of Italian Baroque found expression in the *Giardinetto*, or small garden, ring. Its graceful floral patterns suggested romantic trysts, and symbolized the intertwined emotions of lovers wealthy and ardent enough to afford such extravagant displays of passion.

A rich and widely understood language of jewels invested the stones of a ring with huge significance. Each was integrally linked to the nature of love: ruby for ardour, emerald for sincerity, garnet for constancy, amethyst for Venus and a diamond for the incorruptibility of marriage. The enduring quality of diamonds also rendered them a natural choice for the eternity ring, a pledge of commitment after marriage and often associated with the birth of children. Rings may also be very public expressions of love and prestige, as when the Hollywood star Richard Burton gave Elizabeth Taylor the biggest diamond ring in the world at the height of their stage and screen fame. Yet perhaps the rings of greatest significance to their owners are those secretly cherished but never displayed. These are often charged with memories of a love lost through death or circumstance. After his death William of Orange, one of England's less obviously romantic monarchs, was found to be wearing on a ribbon the gold wedding ring that he had given Princess Mary, still entwined with a lock of her hair.

This portrait of Marsilio and his Wife, by the 16th-century Italian artist Lorenzo Lotto, depicts the betrothal of a wealthy young bourgeois couple. Cupid, the god of love, watches with much satisfaction as a ring is placed on the girl's finger.

THE WEDDING

Only in the 20th century has the question arisen of whether the traditional wedding has anything at all to do with the language of love. In the West, where love is increasingly viewed as a private affair, the more elaborate rituals of marriage may sometimes appear irrelevant to a highly personal emotion. Full-scale wedding ceremonies may seem dominated by embarrassing relatives and over-expensive trappings of material and social status. Yet a traditional wedding continues to capture our imagination, and without doubt it remains the most evocative spectacle in the drama of love.

Wedding presents, such as this 18th-century Greek cushion cover, are traditionally important gifts. They bring good wishes for future prosperity into the couple's new home.

For thousands of years marriage has been a formal rite of passage, made into a piece of high theatre. Earlier societies, to whom order in human society was inseparable from a greater natural harmony, imbued marriage rites with a sacred significance because they seemed to affirm the continuation of life itself. Fertility symbols are present in marriage rituals from very diverse cultures. Among the many examples still found in a traditional Western wedding are tossing the bridal bouquet, showering the couple with confetti and applauding the first cut of the wedding cake. In modern Japan many weddings continue to be solemnized by Shinto priests, or *kannushi*, reflecting the ancient religion's close associations with fertility and renewal.

A Hindu marriage ceremony involves the sacrifice of rice grains and clarified butter — both symbols of fertility and prosperity — to the fire god, Agni, who witnesses the couple's vows. In the Hindu tradition the marriage sacrament, or *vivaha*, is recognized as one of the four great life-stages, introducing the shared responsibilities of bearing and raising children. A formal, seven-step dance legalizes the couple's union and emphasizes their hopes for fruitfulness and marital harmony.

Even in a secular context the language of marriage vows is solemn and a failed marriage is still very painful — especially when there are children. The English poet Walter de la Mare

FROM "THE BRIDE"

At last the world says yes;
It wishes me roses and sons.
My friends stand shyly at the door,
Carrying love gifts.

Chemises in cellophane,
Plates, flowers, lace ...
They kiss my cheeks, they marvel
I'm to be a wife.

Bella Akhmadulina, trs from the Russian
by Stephan Stepanchev

Inviting relations and friends to a wedding banquet is an age-old tradition that occurs in most world cultures. Botticelli's The Wedding Feast *shows an elaborate, open-air meal where men and women are seated at opposite tables.*

perceived the power of the emotional bonds that it creates: "The bridge between 'single' and 'married' spans life's most crucial Rubicon. It is one singularly easy to cross, but not to retraverse." Easier divorce has not made this less true emotionally.

Although the forms and styles of weddings have varied widely to reflect the values of individual societies, their intention remains essentially the same. The union of a couple, often confirmed in a contract of marriage, is surrounded with as much social, religious, magical and legal pomp and circumstance as possible. The laws, duties, vows and customs of these incurably optimistic ceremonies were all designed to make the marriage permanent as well as fruitful — although we all know the inconsistencies of the human heart. Weddings at their best are personal rather than formulaic, welcoming families and friends into shared happiness. The creation of new and delightful forms is a tribute to the human powers of love and imagination.

This woodcut by Eric Gill shows a couple locked in a close embrace. Together they form a heart.

I'd like to live with you

In some small town,

In never-ending twilight

And the endless sounds of bells.

And in the little town's hotel —

The thin chime

Of an antique clock,

Like little drops of time.

And sometimes, evenings, from some attic room,

A flute,

A flute-player by a window

And huge tulips at the windows.

And if you didn't love me, I wouldn't even mind.

Marina Tsvetayeva (1892–1941), untitled extract,

trs from the Russian by Paul Schmidt

ARCHETYPES OF LOVE

Out flew the web and floated wide;
The mirror cracked from side to side.

ALFRED LORD TENNYSON (1809–1892), "THE LADY OF SHALOTT"

According to Carl Jung's theory of the collective unconscious, we inherit cultural archetypes that influence the human psyche because they embody desires and anxieties that remain more or less constant. The traditions of love and the stories told about it in literature, mythology or fairytales may seem remote from modern life. Yet, because they deal with basic emotional preoccupations, we find them convincing and invest them with symbolic power to explain our own feelings to ourselves.

Archetypal stories form a kind of mirror-view of what love is, both dramatizing and resolving its key temptations and challenges. There are dangers, of course, in becoming spellbound by the archetype: Tennyson's Lady of Shalott was forbidden to leave her mirror or the loom on which she wove images based on its reflections. When she turned from the mirror to look at the handsome Lancelot, her idealized world was shattered.

THE GOD OF LOVE

The Roman goddess of love, Venus, was held to be Cupid's mother. He shared her wanton power over human emotions.

The god of love, Eros, was first described by the Greek poet Hesiod in the 8th century BC. One of the earliest gods to emerge from Chaos (according to Hesiod's *Theogany*), Eros was a fundamental principle of life: an inexorable, amoral desire for all things to mingle: "the most beautiful of all the immortal gods, who loosens the limbs and overcomes judgment and wise counsel in the breasts of gods and all humans."

To the Greeks Eros represented the strength and urgency of love, rather than its delicate sensuality and pleasure. These qualities formed the feminine essence of Aphrodite, who featured as the primary deity of love in the great poems of Homer. Plato's *Symposium* reinvested the god with his original authority, but sought to distinguish the spiritual impact of Eros from human sexual passion. The god represented a highly refined and transcendent love, an imaginative ideal that has continued to fascinate and perplex lovers ever since.

Eros later became associated more with the lightning process of "falling in love". An image of cause rather than effect, he was equipped with a bow and arrows of irresistible desire and subsumed into Roman mythology as Venus' son Cupid. No longer a primary creative force, the god of love was often presented as a mischievous boy, loosing off arrows of infatuation without a thought for the feelings of those he wounded. Wilful Cupid was notorious for his lack of discrimination, reflecting a vision of falling in love as an entirely random process. His arbitrariness was often symbolized in medieval art by a blindfold. The "blind bow-boy" described in Shakespeare's *Romeo and Juliet* became a widely accepted image for a rather heartless, cruel and amoral sexual imperative.

Bronzino's An Allegory with Venus and Cupid *depicts the debased god of love as a knowing adolescent, engaged in sensual play with his mother. The painting forms a 16th-century warning of the perils of erotic promiscuity.*

GODDESSES OF LOVE

Goddesses of love are a concept even older than Eros, and have appeared in many mythological forms. Their earliest manifestations were as fertility deities, aspects of the Earth Mother from whom all life derived. The savagery of nature was often reflected in the dual roles of ancient goddesses: Ishtar in Sumeria and Astarte in Phoenicia were both associated with war as well as with the planet Venus and love. The goddess Devi, the oldest in the Hindu pantheon, is still worshipped today as both the provider and destroyer of life. These opposing attributes are reflected in Devi's manifestations as Parvati, the celestial "wife" and lover of Shiva, and the horrific "dark one", Kali.

From Hellenistic times, the Greek god of love, Eros, became subservient to the goddess Aphrodite. He was usually depicted as a mischievous boy.

The world's first love poetry was probably inspired by the Egyptian goddess Hathor. She represented the gentle, creative power of love and fertility, expressed through motherhood as well as sexuality. Greek mythology refined aspects of earlier deities in the enchanting Aphrodite, the enduring archetype of sensual love. Her complex, contradictory character reflected the various moods and emotions experienced in, and aroused by, love. Hesiod celebrated the charm and beauty of this "laughter-loving" goddess, whose influence could be felt in "the whispers of girls, smiles, deceits, sweet pleasure and the gentle delicacy of love." In an alternative guise, as Aphrodite Pandemos, she was married to Hephaestus, the smith of the gods, who symbolized the creative intellect. This version of Aphrodite represented the more sexual aspects of love, implicit in her origins as a fertility deity. Both earthly and celestial, her quixotic nature epitomized the wanton fluctuations of love which have always intrigued the human imagination.

Aphrodite, who became known to the Romans as Venus, is Homer's "sweet and winning goddess" – but she is also jealous and unfaithful. She owns a magic girdle of enticement, yet when she falls in love with the beautiful youth Adonis, and discovers that he is immune to its magic, she reveals herself as possessive and demanding. The goddess has been the archetype of female beauty ever since the 4th century BC when the sculptor

MADRIGAL 52

Diana, naked in the shadowy pool,
Brought no more rapture to the greedy eyes
Of him who watched her splashing in the cool
Than did my glimpse of a maiden unaware
Washing a snood, the gossamer garment of
My lady's wild and lovely golden hair;
Wherefore, although the sky burnt hot above,
I shake and shiver with a chill of love.

Francesco Petrarch (1304–74),
trs from the Italian by Morris Bishop

Praxiteles created the sensuous *Cnidian Aphrodite*. Attended by the Three Graces, her gentle and smiling handmaidens, she is anything but gentle in her treatment of mortals who have offended her. She punishes Hippolytus for worshipping her rival, Artemis, by making his stepmother, Phaedra, fall disastrously in love with him.

Like all Greek myths, the stories of Aphrodite depict human passions played out on a heroic scale. The goddess of love has needed through history to be more than a beautiful and virtuous ideal. She has also had to account for the cruelties of love, and to assume some of the burden of guilt for the personal betrayals, adulteries and strange lusts that are often interwoven with human desire.

Botticelli's The Birth of Venus *portrays one version of the goddess's origin — that she was born from the delicate sea foam and washed ashore at Paphos.*

123

LOVE AND MAGIC

The powerful impact of love has always seemed magical in its blinding suddenness and intensity. Romantics through the generations have wanted to believe that their love is somehow predetermined or ordained. Once lovers could no longer place their faith in Cupid or the gods of love, they chose astrology, magic or fate — the Arab *kismet* — to give their choices mystical confirmation.

Literature tells us again and again that love's tragedies are predestined. What chance had the star-crossed lovers, Romeo and Juliet? In the great medieval love cycle of Tristan and Isolde, what alternatives were open to them? As Tristan brought Isolde to her wedding with his uncle and lord, King Mark of Cornwall, the unhappy couple were accidentally served a magic love potion, intended to bring the future husband and wife "one life, one death, one joy, one sorrow". Instead, it bound Tristan and Isolde in guilty love, treachery, anguished separations, secret reunions and eventual death. The fatal potion is a metaphor for the overwhelming impact of love and desire. Its magic is denied by the 20th-century writer Laurence Binyon in a moving celebration of the power of love itself: "No stealth of a drop distilled / By a spell in the night, no art / No charm, could have ever filled / With aught but thee my heart."

Folklore and fairytales also seek to provide magical explanations for love's mysteries. Their basis is often wish-fulfilment. The miracle-working djinni of

A sorceress weaves a spell to draw her lover to her in a 15th-century German painting, The Magic of Love. *For centuries lovers have believed that magical potions could help them to achieve their desire.*

Arabian tales, uncoiling from a rubbed lamp, has a clear erotic significance. Unconscious or conscious desires — particularly if they involve social taboos — have always been expressed in stories of sorcery, enchantment, shape-changing and the breaking of physical laws. Events in these tales, full of psychological significance, unfold as in a dream, where we fall in love or are loved with startling ease.

Love at first sight may be a magical transformation or a comic delusion. Shakespeare mocks its effect in *A Midsummer Night's Dream* when Oberon claims that the juice of the flower called love-in-idleness, rubbed on the eyelids, "Will make or man or woman madly dote / Upon the next live creature that it sees". Titania's ensuing passion for Bottom the weaver, who has been magically endowed with an ass's head, parodies the wilful delusions of lovers who have fallen into passion's snare. However, the idea that love can be influenced by herbs or potions, aphrodisiacs, spells, or ruling stars, has been slow to disappear. The mysterious progress of love, it seems, is too important to be left to human whims, and, as Hermia says in *A Midsummer Night's Dream*, fate alone can achieve its resolution: "If then true lovers have been ever cross'd / It stands as an edict in destiny ... / As due to love as thoughts and dreams and sighs, / Wishes and tears, poor fancy's followers."

The secular, sceptical, modern age still retains its fascination with the mystery of the heart. Whether seeking compatibility in the signs of the Zodiac or using the traditional magic of herbs to reinvigorate desire, today's lovers respond to the irrational power of an emotion that continues to defy logic or control.

Mythological creatures were often blamed for the abduction or betrayal of a loved one. Gustav Klimt's painting The Sea Serpent *portrays a woman ensnared in a sea monster's embrace.*

THE POWER OF BEAUTY

Beauty has inspired a range of ambivalent feelings over the centuries, from devotion to suspicion, anguish to delight. Its impact on the human imagination is enormous, investing the possessor with great emotional power. A lovely lyric poem by Wallace Stevens, "The Plot Against the Giant", describes how three girls plan to use the most subtle means possible to gain control over their opponent. One of the trio declares: "I shall run before him, / Arching cloths besprinkled with colours / As small as fish eggs. / The threads will abash him." Delicacy and grace are perceived to be more than a match for mere masculine strength.

When they are combined with true physical beauty, there is no longer a contest: beauty conquers all.

The potential danger of female beauty, as well as the passions it can inspire, is epitomized in myth by the figure of Helen of Troy. According to Homer's epic poem *The Iliad*, her loveliness provided the catalyst for a long and destructive war between Greece and Troy. The goddesses Aphrodite, Athene and Hera all claimed a golden apple dedicated to "the most beautiful", and were vain enough to submit to a beauty contest judged by the young Trojan prince Paris. Beset with tempting offers from each contender, Paris awarded the apple to Aphrodite, the goddess of love, who promised to give him the most beautiful woman in the world. Aphrodite helped Paris to persuade Helen, the queen of Sparta, to abandon her husband and flee with Paris to Troy. After ten years of

Although concepts of beauty change with each generation, the ancient Greek theory of an Ideal Beauty has dominated Western culture for the last 2,000 years. Sir Frank Dicksee's portrait, Miranda, *shows a 19th-century English society lady dressed as a Greek goddess.*

This Indian miniature shows the god Krishna dazzled as Radha reveals her beautiful face.

My love in her attire doth show her wit,
It doth so well become her;
For every season she hath dressings fit,
For Winter, Spring and Summer.
No beauty she doth miss
When all her robes are on:
But Beauty's self she is
When all her robes are gone.

Anonymous,
17th-century madrigal

conflict the avenging Greek fleets destroyed Troy and all of its inhabitants.

This story of almost three thousand years ago is an epic metaphor for the ambivalent relationship of beauty and love, and the destruction that it can create within a marriage. Great beauty may inspire desire, jealousy or betrayal; it can provoke rivalry, disharmony and war. Historically, the impact of beauty has turned politicians and soldiers from the path of duty and determined the fate of whole kingdoms and empires. "Had Cleopatra's nose been a little shorter, the whole face of the world might have been changed," wrote the French philosopher Blaise Pascal.

Pascal touches here on a truth about beauty — that its ultimately mysterious power can depend upon an irresistible detail. The power of both male and female beauty depends on personality, as well as on prevailing cultural and aesthetic fashions. We have only to compare the rounded stomachs, thin arms and small breasts of medieval beauties with Rubens' paintings of full-breasted, heavy-bodied goddesses to see that ideas of beauty change. What is constant about beauty is its desirability and the fascination it exerts over the beholder who feels its spell. "If ever any beauty I did see," wrote John Donne, "Which I desired and got / 'twas but a dream of thee."

Antonio Correggio's Jupiter and Io *depicts the story of the beautiful priestess of Argos who was loved by Jupiter (Zeus). The god changed her into a heifer in an attempt to shield her from the envy of his wife Juno (Hera).*

THE COURTESAN

Manet's uncompromising painting Olympia, depicting a prostitute and her black maid, caused a scandal in the French art world when it was exhibited at the Paris Salon of 1865. The model's bold, provocative gaze challenged the viewer with an assertion of her confident sexuality.

The courtesan might seem at first to represent the antithesis of love, but in many ways her history is spectacularly romantic. From the *hetairae* of ancient Greece to the hugely powerful mistresses of 17th-century kings, courtesans have been the objects of idealized love and high emotion. Historically, many received the love that was absent from aristocratic marriages of convenience — though love was clearly not all, nor even the main thing, that men sought in these liaisons.

The true courtesan was traditionally far more than a beautiful prostitute. In the Floating World of 17th-century Japan, the *oiran* or senior courtesans were highly educated women, expertly tutored in music and poetry, as well as in the arts of love-making. The Greek *hetairae* were permitted to mix socially with men and frequently held far more influence over them than did their wives. Xenophon, the Greek philosopher, claimed that the *hetaira* Diotima taught him what he knew of higher love, while another, Phryne, is cited by Plutarch as a renowned enchantress who inspired, among many others, the celebrated sculptor, Praxiteles. Catullus's most moving poems are those dedicated to "Lesbia", thought to be a pseudonym for Clodia Metelli, the famously wanton wife of a Roman governor.

Courtesans may have left abandoned wives — and in some societies their own husbands — in their wake, but these women often commanded intense love and prompted great works of art, from the tragic heroine of Verdi's opera *La Traviata* to Manet's fascinating portrait of the haughty, naughty French cocotte whom he named Olympia.

Many of the most successful courtesans in history were cultured and

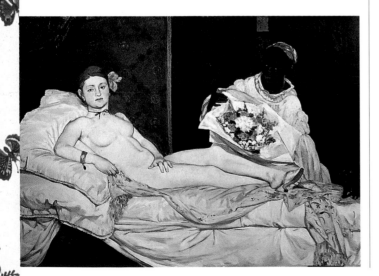

In pre-Islamic Assyria, Persia and Egypt most royal courts possessed a harem, consisting of the ruler's wife, concubines and attendants. A harem could become a highly political forum if its inhabitants competed for power and influence.

Kitagawa Utamaro's 18th-century woodblock print, Lovers, *is one in a series of remarkable portraits of Japanese women. At the height of his career Utamaro produced some prints of the wife and concubines of Toyotomi Hideyoshi, the military ruler. Accused of insulting the ruler's dignity, he was handcuffed for 50 days.*

sophisticated, enjoying considerable power and prestige. Roxelana Sultan, allegedly once a Russian slave, ended her 16th-century career by ruling the harem of Suleiman the Magnificent and advising the Ottoman ruler in his war against the Egyptian sultanate. Famous among the *cortegiane* of the Italian Renaissance was the poet Tullia d'Aragona, a woman whose philosophical writings engaged men's minds while her striking eyes captured their hearts. In France, extraordinary women such as La Pompadour and Diane de Poitiers captivated kings and used the power of love to influence the unfolding of history itself.

THE THREE-FACED

Who calls her two-faced? Faces she has three:
The first inscrutable, for the outer world;
The second shrouded in self-contemplation;
The third, her face of love,
Once for an endless moment turned on me.

Robert Graves (1895–1985)

THE IMAGE OF DESIRE

Discovering and falling in love with the man or woman of our dreams is not so common as we may wish to believe. Even if adolescents do form their own "love-map", it is seldom very detailed – and may be wildly impractical! A more mature view of love is less inclined to describe the precise image of our desire and accept no compromise. Yet the romantic search for a preconceived ideal continues to attract our imagination and to dominate fairytale themes. If the ideal is not available, myths have often explored the possibility of creating it.

Ovid's story of Pygmalion describes the imaginative impulse to mould a love object to one's own desire. The sculptor Pygmalion, disgusted by the wanton behaviour of the women of Cyprus, had sworn never to marry. He poured his longing for a purer beauty into carving an ivory statue of a woman. Pygmalion's creation assumed a form so lovely and lifelike that he promptly fell in love with her. He clothed the statue, laid her on feather pillows, brought gifts of shells, pebbles, birds, flowers and amber, and caressed her with such passion that

Aubrey Beardsley's illustration of the Bible story of Salome and King Herod was created for Oscar Wilde's play, Salome, *published in 1894. Wilde's complex, disturbing version of the story describes Salome's passion for John the Baptist, which becomes murderous when her ideal spurns her love.*

he was afraid to bruise her limbs. Venus, the Roman goddess of love, heard his prayers and took pity on him. The ivory softened and grew warm, veins throbbed at his kiss and the statue's eyes opened.

George Bernard Shaw's famed comedy of *Pygmalion* brought the fable to life in an early 20th-century setting. Eliza Doolittle, a London flower-girl, is successfully moulded into a splendid lady by the egotistical Professor Higgins. However, she finally informs him that she has outgrown his experiment and intends to make a life of her own. This psychologically convincing ending is characteristic of such love affairs. They often founder on the narcissism of the dominant partner, who only loves what he has created and resents any assertion of will and individual identity. The musical version, *My Fair Lady*, returned to Ovid's more popular, less plausible ending.

The great theatre for Pygmalion-style love affairs is provided by the world of entertainment itself. Traditionally, in this artificial environment, young stars

Jean-Léon Gérome's painting Pygmalion and Galatea *captures the sensual, miraculous moment when the statue of Galatea comes to life and kisses her sculptor.*

The 20th century has created enormously powerful icons of desire from film stars and pop musicians. Andy Warhol's image of Marilyn Monroe, the most enduring of all Hollywood's sex symbols, has achieved celebrity status in its own right.

are not born but made, as their names, bodies and personae are reshaped by older, more experienced men. Maurice Stiller, for example, was 41 when he met the 18-year-old who became Greta Garbo; Carlo Ponti met the 16-year-old Sophia Loren when he was 37. The former relationship was short-lived, yet the latter, perhaps surprisingly, endured.

Our modern images of desire are often film or pop stars. Redirecting our desire to a real person in the everyday world – where people have flaws and things can go wrong – is a significant stage in emotional development. Yet we are all Pygmalions to a degree: falling in love would be impossible without some conception of what we believe the other to be. It takes flexibility and tolerance to allow the image of desire to reshape itself into complex reality.

THE VIRGIN AND THE UNICORN

One of the paradoxes of deep human love is that it represents an imaginative synthesis of spiritual and sensual desires. For centuries, this apparent contradiction led the Christian moralists to argue that all carnal love was sinful except as a means of procreation within lawful marriage.

This detail from The Lady and the Unicorn, *a 15th-century tapestry, shows the mythological beast lying in the lap of the virgin, looking at his reflection in an upheld mirror.*

Out of the struggle to reconcile sexuality with purity emerged the beautiful and poetic legend of the virgin and the unicorn. The medieval symbol of pure love was a beast of fable — a graceful white animal resembling the oryx antelope of Arabia, with a spiral horn on its forehead, the maned head and body of a horse, the hoofs of an antelope and the tail of a lion. By the 15th century, when the famous group of tapestries of *The Lady and the Unicorn* were made for Jean le Viste, duc d'Arcy, the symbol had been elaborated into a complex allegory of spiritualized love. The sexual convention of the male hunting the desired female was reversed, and erotic love was sublimated into tenderness. The elusive and fierce unicorn with its phallic horn could be captured only by a virgin, in whose lap it would quietly rest its head.

At a secular level, the unicorn embodies male strength, freedom and virility. It consents to submit to the maiden as the conventions of courtly love required the knight to surrender his heart and autonomy to his lady. However, at the heart of the fable is a more enduring idea: that goodness has an essential power over wildness, and that love can refine and control emotions as well as inflame them.

In medieval times the unicorn became a metaphor for the penetrating sweetness of the Holy Spirit, while the lady represented the Virgin Mary herself. A pagan interpretation viewed her as the cool, chaste huntress Artemis or Diana — a virginal beauty to be worshipped but never possessed.

THE BEAST ADORED

One of the most compelling and poignant love stories ever written is the fable of Beauty and the Beast, made famous in the version by Madame Leprince de Beaumont in 1757. Its young heroine, aptly named Beauty, agrees to enter a monster's castle as hostage for her father. The monster falls in love with her and begins to pine when she shrinks from him in horror. Finding him kind, and pitying his anguish, she eventually kisses him — to discover that he is really a fine prince.

The Beast is a recurrent feature of fairytales, where appearances are often set at variance with reality. In another manifestation he is the loathsome Frog Prince, able to escape from his repulsive outer skin only by the willingness of another to see beneath it. As the English moralist G. K. Chesterton perceived, the truth that such tales disclose "is that a thing must be loved before it is lovable". Our attractiveness is redefined by the response in a lover's gaze: to see only coldness or revulsion there, as the Beast initially does, is emotionally devastating.

Yet the power of the archetype — and the reason why it endures as a modern myth — lies in a universal longing to be loved for what we are, rather than how we outwardly appear. In Edmond Rostand's play *Cyrano de Bergerac*, this theme is given a cruelly ironic twist. Cyrano, the hero, is a brilliant, sensitive man, but a shy

The daughter of the king of Tyre, Europa was abducted by Zeus in the form of a bull. She was carried away to Crete, where she bore three sons. Among the many illustrations of the story are Francesci's The Rape of Europa *(above) and Henri Fuseli's* Europa and the Bull *(below).*

FROM "LEDA AND THE SWAN"

A sudden blow: the great wings beating still
Above the staggering girl, her thighs caressed
By the dark webs, her nape caught in his bill,
He holds her helpless breast upon his breast.

How can those terrified vague fingers push
The feathered glory from her loosening thighs?
And how can body, laid in that white rush,
But feel the strange heart beating where it lies?

W. B. Yeats (1865-1939)

---

and ugly lover, possessed of a peculiarly dominant nose. Believing his own suit to be hopeless, he agrees to write love letters to his adored Roxane on behalf of a good-looking, apparently more worthy rival. Cyrano later learns that Roxane fell in love with the writer of the letters and not the face of her young suitor. Only as he is dying Cyrano does admit his authorship, knowing that, despite physical ugliness, his innermost self has been truly beloved.

Pity for an object of revulsion, such as the Hunchback of Notre-Dame or Dr Frankenstein's monster in Mary Shelley's novel, counterpoints the adolescent longing for an abstract ideal. In evoking human sympathy for all that falls short of perfection, we hope that a caring face of love may overlook our own deficiencies.

Stories in which the Beast is animalistic have a different, more disturbing

Marc Chagall's painting A Midsummer Night's Dream *illustrates the play's themes of illusion, magic and love. Titania, queen of the fairies, is bewitched into believing that Bottom the weaver, who has the head of an ass, is beautiful.*

subtext. In the classic film *King Kong*, the contrast between Fay Wray's helpless delicacy and the gorilla's brutish passion contains a strong erotic charge. From the satyrs of Greek mythology onwards, the Beast has been a recurring symbol of male lust, which may simultaneously attract and repel. The dark, brooding heroes of romantic fiction refine the archetype, but retain the power of its underlying sexuality; clean-cut looks and well-mannered charm can seem bland in comparison. Confronted by the wooden handsomeness of Jean Marais at the dénouement of Jean Cocteau's film version of *Beauty and the Beast*, Greta Garbo famously exclaimed to the director: "Give me back my Beast!"

THE OBSTACLE

The love of Mars, the god of war, and Venus, the goddess of love, was often depicted in the Renaissance by artists such as Mantegna. They believed that Harmony was born of the union between Love and Strife.

If there is one overriding message in all the writing on love, it is that achieving true love is a battle. Every lover, said Ovid, is a soldier, and love for centuries has been considered a prize to be fought for. There are no couples in literature — or at least none whom we care to remember — who have not had to confront obstacles, sometimes terrible ones, in order to be together.

Recent history includes two powerful stories of love that provoked divided loyalties. On January 30, 1889, the young Archduke Rudolph, the Crown Prince of Austria, was found dead at his hunting lodge of Mayerling, shot by his own revolver. Beside him was the body of the Baroness Maria Vetsera, aged only 18. The Crown

Prince appears to have chosen death rather than remain torn between his marriage and his love for Maria Vetsera, and it seems that she chose to die with him. "Forgive me for what I have done," she wrote to her mother, "I could not resist love." No more, 50 years later, could the British king Edward VIII, enthralled by the American Wallis Simpson. In Britain a constitutional crisis ensued over his wish to marry a divorcee; Edward abdicated from the throne in 1936, to be free to marry Wallis and live with her abroad in self-imposed exile.

Modern lovers may not have to choose between their kingdoms and their love, and may rarely have occasion to risk death for each other. However, dramatic stories of lovers' obstacles continue to fascinate us, being idealizations of our own experience. We have all known the heightening of emotion when love is obstructed, and the irony that love often becomes clearly defined for us only after it has been somehow thwarted.

Literature has dramatized the trials of love in a myriad different ways, from the metaphorical briar thickets in the path of suitors to the material impediments of money, or constraints of social class (which separated Heathcliff from Cathy in *Wuthering Heights*). Differences of politics may also impinge on lovers: Boris Pasternak's novel *Dr Zhivago* describes the tragic division of Lara and Zhivago by the ideological hatreds of civil war following the Russian Revolution.

Opposition by parents has been a consistent theme in the trials of young lovers since Ovid's tale of Pyramus and Thisbe. These two lovers defy their parents by talking through a crack in the wall between their houses, before the mistaken belief that Thisbe is dead causes Pyramus to kill himself. The story of Romeo and Juliet, who are fatally divided by the family feuds of Montague and Capulet, has come to exemplify star-crossed lovers everywhere. Modern political or religious tensions have generated yet further occasions to illustrate this age-old theme. Emotional pressure to keep a child, particularly a daughter, at home may prove another obstacle to successful love. It can be exerted by a parent in a variety of subtle ways; for example Mr Woodhouse in Jane Austen's novel *Emma* falls ill with exquisite timing at the prospect of any situation that he might dislike.

Nevertheless, love continues to survive and even to thrive on its obstacles. Young lovers still defy their parents to elope, or at least dream of it. Other affairs are simply, and tragically, overwhelmed before they begin by the small misdirections of fate, recalled with haunting clarity by the Greek poet C.P. Cavafy:

> Body remember, not only how much you
> were loved,
> not only the beds you lay on,
> but also those desires glowing openly
> in eyes that looked at you,
> trembling for you in voices —
> only some chance obstacle frustrated them.

The possibility of parental deception, in a society that allowed most unmarried women little personal freedom, is the subject of the painting Trust Me, *by the Pre-Raphaelite artist Sir John Everett Millais.*

Evelyn de Morgan's 19th-century painting Hero Awaiting the Return of Leander *portrays the Greek myth of the ill-fated priestess. Her lover Leander swam across the Hellespoint from Abydos each night to visit her. One evening a storm put out the light she guided him with, and he was cruelly drowned.*

THE PRISONER IN THE TOWER

This Bengali painting shows a couple attempting to elope together on the back of an elephant.

The image of a beautiful woman imprisoned in a tower is a recurrent motif in art and literature. Carl Jung identified it as one of the most fundamental of all psychological archetypes. It symbolized for him every man's unconscious search for his own *anima* — the female side of the male psyche. By falling in love, men sought to discover a projection of their own *anima* — the princess in the tower.

However, the image also has a wider symbolism. The tower itself is perceived as a male emblem of ambition, aspiration or ascent; in terms of love, it may also portray female purity and inaccessibility. In art, the woman in a tower or castle specifically symbolizes chastity — especially in cultures where female virtue was fiercely protected.

In the great medieval allegory *The Romance of the Rose*, the lover had to attack the Castle of Love to pick his rosebud and achieve his heart's desire. The allegorical Castle of Love was often guarded by Jealousy. Both in fairytales and in real life, medieval women could be imprisoned in remote castles by rich, elderly husbands as a punishment for actual or imagined infidelities.

The implication of the archetype was that the prisoner in the tower must wait passively for deliverance, rather than take any initiative herself. The modern modification of this idea is described in D. H. Lawrence's novel *The Rainbow*, where it reflects the growing maturity of the heroine. Entranced as a young girl by the story of Elaine, aloof from the world and loyally guarding Lancelot's shield, the adult Ursula has the confidence to leave her imaginary tower behind and, like a modern girl, go looking for love.

In mythology, towers are closely linked with female chastity,
either self-imposed or enforced by others — a state from which the heroine is usually rescued.

THE KNIGHT

The knight in shining armour has been one of the most enduring of all love archetypes – perhaps because it responds to certain desires in both women and men. Its greatest exemplar, Lancelot of the Lake, was as brave and adventurous as any man could wish to be. Yet he was also utterly ruled by love – so enthralled by Queen Guinevere that he would face any danger, accept any humiliation and betray any loyalty except to her.

Lancelot is a figure straight out of the courtly love traditions of 12th-century France. The long poem by Chrétien de Troyes that celebrates his exploits was written under the patronage of a woman – Marie, Comtesse de Champagne. Thus the knight of romantic tradition, at least in his origins, was not simply the male power fantasy to which he is sometimes reduced – a conquering hero riding around rescuing damsels in distress. Lancelot's freedom of action was in fact deeply compromised by his love for Guinevere, the wife of his own lord. She was the controlling force in his life, and seems to have enjoyed her power, putting his love to

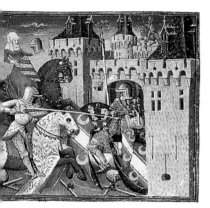

Lancelot of the Lake, seen here capturing a castle, was presented in Arthurian romance as the model of chivalry, bravery and fidelity. However, his adultery with Guinevere, the wife of the king he loved, led to the destruction of the Round Table civilization and the death of Arthur.

rather cruel or arbitrary tests. "The knight departing for new adventures offends his lady, but she has nothing but contempt for him if he remains at her feet," observed Simone de Beauvoir.

The image of the knight has assumed many different forms since early medieval romances. Cervantes' novel *Don Quixote* parodies the unreal idealism of the knightly code through its charming but incompetent anti-hero. Nor was it solely a male preserve. The ambivalent figure of the female knight in Renaissance poetry exploited the contrast between steely armour and soft, milky limbs for a powerful erotic charge.

The romantic figure of the male knight was much admired in the 19th century for his associated virtues of courage, honour and courtesy to the ladies in his charge. In Britain this was expressed in the work of Pre-Raphaelite painters, highly influenced by Arthurian legends, and of poets such as Alfred, Lord Tennyson. The passive role of women in many such tales – beautiful,

In the classic 1942 film Casablanca, Humphrey Bogart plays Rick, a bruised idealist haunted by the bitter-sweet memory of a fleeting Paris romance with Ilse (Ingrid Bergman). Rick saves the lives of the girl and her husband at great personal cost.

imperilled, but dependent on a male to rescue and protect them — may reflect contemporary male unease about the growing demands of women for more economic and social freedom.

Nowadays the theme of rescue has begun to look archaic, as more equal relationships assume an ideal of mutual support and assistance. Yet as a figure of faithful love and resourceful courage, the knight is unlikely to disappear from romantic tradition. Who was the shadowy figure behind Humphrey Bogart in *Casablanca* or Gary Cooper in *High Noon* if not a modern knight errant?

Paolo Uccello's St George *and the* Dragon *depicts the patron saint of England slaughtering the dragon to release the captive maiden — a theme recurring in countless fairytales and myths.*

141

GARDENS OF THE SENSES

The garden has presented lovers throughout history with an extraordinarily sensual setting. A real garden is already a world apart, an idealization of nature placed within a defining frame. Into this perfect romantic space, writers and artists have poured their complex, ambivalent allegories of Eden, of innocence and temptation, of pastoral bliss and erotic sensuousness. Poets have borrowed the imagery of gardens and nature to evoke the blossoming of love (and its ephemerality) and the fertility of women, or simply to celebrate true physical beauty. ("She opened her eyes," wrote D. H. Lawrence, "and green / They shone clear like flowers undone / For the first time, now for the first time seen.") Such images reveal the romantic power of the real garden, stocked with the symbolic allusions of religion and mythology and subconsciously making Adams and Eves of us all.

An Indian miniature painting of a prince and his mistress, c.1780. The Mughal emperors brought a sensual, secular tradition of garden allegory to India. This lush scene, with its plump plantains, inviting pavilion and pair of Brahminy ducks, is an appropriate setting for the enrapt lovers.

This medieval walled garden, in a 15th-century manuscript, presents an allegory of earthly delights recalling the biblical Eden.

The atmosphere of a garden may be innocent or libidinous, pastoral or exotic. In the Judeo-Christian world-view, the idealized garden is the biblical one of chastity — Eden before the Fall, or the closed garden described in the Bible's Song of Songs: "a garden locked is my sister, my bride". The Song of Songs is itself a poetic evocation of the ancient walled gardens of Persia, and the Arabic word for paradise is

al-janna, the garden. In secular art and poetry, the garden provides a scene for enchanting, perhaps overwhelming, the senses. The sexual imperative is manifest within the natural world: flowers, insects and birds reproduce themselves as part of a greater, exhilarating life force. Yet in the creation of a harmonious garden, wilder forces are restrained; order and sophistication have triumphed, allowing graceful dalliance and elegant games to be indulged as elaborate, protracted courtship rituals. In medieval courtly romances, such as *The Romance of the Rose*, the garden becomes an elegant battleground in the struggle for virtue. Three centuries later, life imitated art: the Cardinal of Ferrara's garden at the Villa d'Este in Italy offered a moral trial for visitors, who could choose paths leading either to Virtue or Pleasure.

The role of the garden in medieval romance is more than symbolic. It afforded welcome respite from the crowded communal life indoors, and the sense of retreat into a private, sensually charged space that reflected the psychological impact of a burgeoning love affair. In the new designs of the Renaissance, gardens became elaborately styled playgrounds, in which hidden water jets could surprise lovers — who in turn could surprise each other, as Jane Eyre is later to discover when Rochester proposes to her in the garden at Thornfield. As modern lovers stroll through rose walks or kiss behind hedges, they are influenced by the weight of romantic allusion, as well as by the sights and scents around them.

This French snuff box of 1749 is decorated with exotic pinks — a symbol of betrothal, and a popular emblem on lovers' gifts.

This Renaissance painting shows Flora, Roman goddess of flowers. She enjoyed perpetual spring in a garden of flowers and fruit, where the Graces twined garlands for their hair. Here, though, she reclines in a formal setting in the Italianate style.

Sensuous women
in summer love
weave
flower earrings
from fragile petals
of mimosa
while wild bees
kiss them gently.

from *Sakuntala*,
a 5th-century Sanskrit play

THE MYSTIC ROSE

The pre-eminence of the rose as a love symbol goes back to antiquity when it was sacred to deities of love, especially the Greek goddess Aphrodite. Her priestesses wore white roses (emblems of virginity) and the paths of her shrines were strewn with rose petals. Together with its Eastern equivalent, the lotus, the flower became an enduring symbol of both human and spiritual desire, acquiring deeper mystical significance over time. The folded bud became a metaphor for the heart. The opening petals were an allegory, not only of birth and the source of life, but also of spiritual growth. In Tantric Buddhism, the fusion of sexual and spiritual aspiration is described as "the jewel in the lotus". Christianity was slower to accept the rose as a comparable symbol of human and divine love, and it was only in the 13th century that an influential allegory of the mystic rose, *The Romance of the Rose*, appeared.

This voluminous poem, begun by Guillaume de Lorris in 1236 and greatly lengthened by Jean de Meun 40 years later, depicts the art of love as a discipline beset with obstacles and difficulties, requiring the slow development of self-knowledge. The young hero passionately desires to pick a rosebud (the innermost self of his beloved) in the garden of love, but discovers that he must endure many frustrations before he can achieve this. In one of the poem's key passages, he looks into the Spring of Narcissus in which two crystals refract images of himself and of the rosebud. His need to perfect himself if he wishes to attain the Other illustrates how inextricably Love and Christian goodness are mingled.

The mystique of the rose is deeply ambiguous — by turns romantic, sacred and erotic. The rose symbolizes the fountain of God's bounty, the glory of Nature itself, the beauty of the beloved and the fruitful promise of human love. An image of an earthly paradise, a rose garden may also represent the rosary — literally a garden of prayers to the Virgin Mary, the Rose of Heaven. Christ's heart, too, is a rose on fire with love, the thorns a symbol of his Passion.

Carnally the red rose is a highly charged image of sexual arousal, and of the vulva itself. Its scent, the secret ingredient of perfumes through the centuries, is a powerful aphrodisiac, as Cleopatra knew when she entertained Mark Antony in a room deep in rose petals. Little wonder that love can be declared by a single bloom.

Different coloured roses
have different meanings.
The yellow rose signifies
jealousy or infidelity, the
white rose suggests youth
and purity, and the red
rose is for passion.

Many medieval
depictions of courtly love
are staged in gardens,
which had Christian
as well as sensual
connotations.

Towards the end of
The Romance of the
Rose the hero-poet,
after undergoing a series
of trials, attains the rose
of his choice.

145

THE KISS

Perhaps nowhere else is the poverty of a dictionary definition so exposed as in its description of a kiss: a touch or pressure given with the lips in token of affection, greeting or reverence. The kiss of lovers, of course, is infinitely more than this, as the American poet Robert Frost expresses in a poem infused with nostalgic memories of his youth: "Love at the lips was touch / As sweet as I could bear."

The erotic kiss is a psychological moment of enormous power which, for lovers, redefines all that went before. A kiss can appear to suspend time, to make the world dip out of sight, only to return transformed. We exchange the breath of life when we kiss lip to lip or nose to nose, as in the kisses of Maori and Eskimo people. The kiss is an act of union, and recognized as such in religious and secular contexts.

In fairytales, the kiss changes all. It is the defining moment in many of these stories, which treat through metaphor the awakening of sexual consciousness. Sleeping Beauty, Snow White and Wagner's sleeping Brunhilde are all awakened with a kiss from their long, pre-adolescent slumbers. For novelists depicting Western courtship, the first kiss of lovers may be a moment of exquisite, sometimes cataclysmic, intensity, heightened by delay. In Emily Brontë's classic novel *Wuthering Heights*, Heathcliff waits four years to kiss Cathy, and then "neither spoke, nor loosed his hold for some five minutes, during

Auguste Rodin's ability to produce extraordinarily lifelike statues gave rise to the unfounded rumour that he cast his bronzes from live models. The Kiss, a remarkably sensitive and sensuous work, carved in marble, silenced his critics.

Pablo Picasso's 20th-century representation of the kiss, painted towards the end of his life, shows the powerful charge and confusion that can result from an embrace.

which period he bestowed more kisses than ever he gave in his life before."

The erotic power of the kiss links two people so closely that it has an inherent privacy about it. Its essence is famously captured in one of the most unforgettable images in art — Rodin's sculpture of *The Kiss*. His marble couple seem so lost in each other that the viewer cannot intrude upon them, no matter from which angle the sculpture is seen.

The kiss, so simple and yet so utterly transforming, will always be more than the sum of its parts. The song in *Casablanca*, one of the most romantic films ever made, may claim that "A kiss is just a kiss, a sigh is just a sigh", but, as lovers everywhere know, this uniquely human gesture can celebrate both tenderness and passion in a single, extraordinary moment.

The Kiss *by Edvard Munch expresses the sense of silence and stillness that can occur when you kiss a loved one for the first time.*

O the water of love

that floods everything over, so that there is

nothing the eye sees that is not covered in.

There is no angle

the world can assume which the love in my

eye cannot make into a symbol of love.

Even the precise geometry

of his hand, when I gaze at it,

dissolves me into water and I flow away in

a flood of love.

Elizabeth Smart (1913–86), *By Grand Central Station I Sat Down and Wept*

THE NIGHT OF LOVE

In this morning scene a man is preparing to leave his lover, who is lying in glorious aban-don on the bed. Clothes strewn hastily on the floor are further evidence of a night of passion.

Lovers have always laid claim to the night as their own — a world apart, separate from the mundane complexities of the day. This belief, reflected in love songs and poems across centuries, perceives night as an ally of lovers, part of their conspiracy of concealment. "The night was made for loving," wrote Byron, and Shakespeare's Juliet calls on the "love-producing night" to "spread thy close curtain". The lover in John Donne's famous poem "The Sunne Rising" tries to prolong the night by ordering away the sun: "Busie old foole, unruly Sunne / Why dost thou thus / Through windowes and through cur-taines call on us? / Must to thy motions lovers' seasons run?"

Yet dawn must inevitably return, bringing with it, for lovers, the fear that the delights of the past night will prove no more than an illusion. Women through history have feared, and found, that when the tasks of the day regain the man's attention, he will abandon them and withdraw into the "rational" world.

The Arabian fairytale of *The Thousand and One Nights* dramatizes these fears of male betrayal. It tells the story of the all-powerful Sultan Schahriah, who has vowed to take a new bride every night, and to have each put to death at dawn, to prevent possible infidelity. However, the charming and intelligent heroine Scheherazade outwits him, surviving each night by telling a compelling story and promising to recount another the next night. After an onerous number of storytelling nights, she persuades the Sultan to revoke his decree and hail her as the liberator of women. This fairytale is an ancient call to arms by women against the purely sexual encounter, an enforced single night of love.

Lovers, *a linocut by John Buckland Wright,*
is a powerful depiction of a couple surrounded
by the flames of their desire.

THE WANDERER

Jean Honoré Fragonard's painting The Rape *illustrates the violence behind some seductions carried out by literary rakes such as Don Juan. Serial lovers may also inflict emotional damage on the objects of their transient affections.*

The idea that love is an amusing and pleasurable game of chase, conquest and skilful disengagement has existed for centuries in very different cultures. It remains a predominantly masculine concept, although the "aggressors" have not always been men nor the "victims" always women. Aspects of physiology as well as social traditions have contributed to the emergence of the wandering rake — an archetypal threat to those seeking an enduring love.

Don Juan towers above other mythic seducers because he embodies several male fantasies on a heroic scale. Since his first appearance in Tirso de Molina's *The Rake of Seville* in 1630, Don Juan has epitomized the charming and profligate deceiver. Able to capture women's hearts almost at will, he nevertheless evades the tedious bonds of faithful love. Although his capacity to sustain relationships is non-existent, the Don's sense of adventure, curiosity, sexual appetite and physical energy are boundless. All this has made him particularly fascinating to male writers, for whom he is perhaps a metaphor for their own creative drive.

Psychotherapists who encounter "Don Juanism" in their patients classify it as an essentially childish and narcissistic condition. The motivations for it are many and varied, but include a boastful attempt to prove virility by purely sexual means, a basic incapacity to love or a present insecurity that refuses to limit future options. It is also a way of avoiding commitment to a long-term partner who might discover weaknesses behind superficial bravado. However, analysis of the somewhat pathetic philanderers of reality shows them to be in strong contrast to the engaging Don Juan in his literary, dramatic and operatic manifestations.

Stendhal, who displays great sensitivity for women in his work, dismissed the Don as "a dishonest trader who takes but never pays". Not surprisingly, Byron took another view. He perceived an attractive adventurer, whose wish to make love to all women rather than just one rendered him a tireless, devoted worshipper at the shrine of the Eternal Feminine.

Rakes must of necessity be well versed in the arts of seduction. Dallying, *by D. Miklos, shows a skilled practitioner murmuring sweet nothings into a receptive feminine ear.*

Molière's Don Juan mockingly stresses the generosity of his indiscriminate attachments. "I am fond of freedom in love ... As soon as a beautiful face asks me for my heart, I would give them all if I had 10,000 hearts." In Mozart's opera *Don Giovanni*, the protagonist is portrayed as a romantic free spirit, whose libertine activities challenge far more than sexual conventions. A charming rebel who is opposed to all limits, human or divine, his defiant courage is overborne at last by a greater, supernatural authority.

Don Juan could not have become a hero without being refreshingly honest about himself. Self-confessed rakes through history have freely admitted to enjoying obstacles as part of the hunt for love. The thrill of encountering a new personality and body fuses with the discovery of a new self through another's eyes. As well as the prestige of conquest, wanderers are able to recapture time and and again the initial passions of love.

A successful philanderer is almost by definition extremely attractive. Skilled in charming others, presenting an irresistible challenge, rakes have always offered a dangerous excitement that transforms an ordinary love affair. Whatever the deplorable morality of the wanderers' conduct, and the emotional chaos that they may cause, they appear never lacking in attentive lovers.

Because of their inability to form lasting relationships, wandering lovers are often alone in the end.

THE MIRRORED SELF

In Aubrey Beardsley's illustration The Mirror of Love *the heart-shaped glass reflects an image of Eros, the god of love.*

To love oneself
is the beginning of a lifelong romance.

OSCAR WILDE (1854–1900)

To some extent, we all resemble Narcissus in Ovid's famous myth — the beautiful youth who pined and died of un-requited love for his own reflection in a pool. With the exception of a partner whom we truly love, nobody is more important to us than ourselves.

The reason Ovid gave for the fate of Narcissus is psychologically penetrating. He had spurned any other love and was punished for it by Nemesis, who heard the cry of a nymph he had curtly rejected: "So may he himself fall in love, so may he himself not be able to possess his beloved!" In other words, self-love can be so strong that we are unable to love anyone else; narcissism is dangerous and ultimately self-destructive.

Narcissism is an element in all human love. It is part of our longing for union with another being, in which identities become subsumed. "I am Heathcliff!" cries the despairing Catherine Earnshaw in *Wuthering Heights*, expressing a feeling that most true lovers have experienced. The sense of loving aspects of oneself as they are perceived in a lover is par-ticularly acute in same-sex relationships, where the adored object is in some ways a mirror image. Narcissus, enraptured by his own youthful beauty, is often held to be an archetype of gay male love. The psychoanalyst Sigmund Freud believed that homosexual relationships derived in part from a search for an idealized version of the ego, or the desire to repossess a youthful self. Accepting a degree of narcissism seems to be an essential part of loving. It can be a subject for comedy, as in Shakespeare's *Much Ado About Nothing*, where the apparently antag-onistic Beatrice and Benedick switch from taunting to loving each other the moment that they hear the other adores them.

THE RAIN PALACE

I have built for you a rain palace
Of alabaster columns and rock crystal
So that a thousand mirrors shall tell me
How ever more beautifully for me you change.

Yvan Goll,
trs from the German by Michael Hamburger

This 16th-century painting of Narcissus shows the beautiful youth gazing at his own reflection in a pool. The love of an image, rather than another being, is ultimately unrewarding, and Narcissus pines away. As he dies he is transformed into the narcissus flower.

The beloved object becomes a reflection of our own attractiveness. In paintings Venus is often portrayed gazing into a mirror, the traditional emblem of love, beauty and happiness. The broken mirror, by contrast, has always symbolized bad luck in love — possibly connected to the ancient belief that the reflection was a twin soul. Narcissus, whose self-love was fatally exclusive, suffered anguish when his reflection broke as he attempted to grasp it in the waters of the pool.

THE DEVOURER

"Heaven has no rage, like love to hatred turned, / Nor hell a fury, like a woman scorned," wrote William Congreve at the turn of the 17th century. He expressed a deep-seated and enduring male fear that love can unleash uncontrollable and destructive emotions in women. Mythology and folklore have created a remarkable gallery of frightening women, governed by the twin passions of jealousy and revenge.

One explanation for this pervasive archetype is its connection with a terrifying mother figure, invested with the power both to create and destroy. These conflicting attributes have been fused in female goddesses for centuries, reflecting the two principles of sex and death on which the natural world depends. The Hindu goddess Devi reveals this dual role in her incarnations as benign Parvati and ferocious Kali. The latter's manifestation as the "dark one", garlanded with skulls and engulfing enemies within a cavernous mouth, emphasizes the sexual aspect of her relentless, terrifying authority.

The female devourer is also integral to Western religious traditions. Many biblical stories feature women who destroy or emasculate men. Judith cuts off the head of the enemy general Holofernes while he sleeps in her arms. Salome, who has charmed Herod with her seductive dancing, demands the head of John the Baptist. Samson's lover Delilah coaxes from him the secret of his superhuman strength — his hair — and tells his enemies to cut it while he sleeps.

Greek mythology contains a variety of avenging, destructive women, who are epitomized by the terrible Furies. Known euphemistically as the Eumenides, or "Kindly Ones", they hound their prey for years to remind them of their guilt. A woman was perceived to pose the greatest threat to a man when he was off-guard and alone — a metaphor for male emotional vulnerability outside the rational world. When the king of Argos, Agamemnon, returns home safely after the

Anthony Sandys' painting Love's Shadow *shows a vengeful-looking woman devouring a posy of flowers, possibly given to her by a lover.*

LIKE GULLIVER

Like Gulliver pulling a hundred ships,
I draw you, my lovers, to the shore,
clumsy, in all colours, cunning with your
tiny swords and shooting from the hips.

Like Gulliver I spare you, even though
you hit my skull cruelly and hope it breaks.
I laugh at you through strings and snakes
of blood, my furious lovers with your tiny bows.

Nina Cassian,
trs from the Romanian by Willis Barnstone
and Matei Calinescu

Trojan Wars, his treacherous queen, Clytemnestra, enmeshes him in a net and murders him. The fearsome Sphinx was a clawed female who waylaid travellers, literally to devour them if they could not answer her riddle. Lamia, a child-killer crazed by the loss of her own children, assumed serpent form and united with the daughters of the witch Hecate, thought to feast on men's blood while they slept. This sexual fear of the draining of vitality found expression in medieval Europe through belief in the succubus, a female demon who lay with sleeping men.

In real life, female agents were often considered "deadlier than the male", particularly where they used sexual wiles to extract information. The German spy Mata Hari, whose name became synonymous with espionage and sexual intrigue early in the 20th century, was as famous for her many celebrated lovers as for the extent of her spying activity.

The devourer seems to feed upon a range of male fears, more varied than a

purely Freudian interpretation might suggest. On one level the archetype embodies male anxieties about the excessive demands of female love, and a corresponding inability to recognize the depths of a woman's passion. This is graphically illustrated in the Greek myth of Medea, one of the most dramatic human avengers. An Asian enchantress, she returns to Greece with Jason after helping him to steal the Golden Fleece from her father. When Jason later abandons her for a Greek woman, Medea murders their two beloved sons in anguished rage. This violent image of a devourer confronts men with the most fearful, nightmarish consequences of love betrayed.

A sense of enchantment runs throughout Keats' poem of betrayed love, La Belle Dame sans Merci, *in which a knight is seduced by a lady in the woods. He falls into a troubled sleep and when he wakes she has gone.*

THE TEMPTRESS

Until the 20th century, women in most societies pinned their hair up when in public, as flowing locks were considered provocative and unruly. This 18th-century Indian miniature shows a woman dressing her hair.

From a modern viewpoint, Adam's part in the Fall seems more duplicitous than Eve's. He ate the forbidden fruit that she offered him, and then blamed his wife for his own wrongdoing. History forgave both his weakness and his disloyalty — and proceeded to confuse the woman with the serpent. The archetype of the temptress was thus established — a dangerous and amoral seducer of men.

Bizet's Carmen is one of the most dramatic examples of a woman who takes the initiative in love, challenging men's traditional right to lead and select. She is a dark, mysterious, fiery creature who whirls the fascinated José from the arms of his kindly, dull, local sweetheart, only to drop him at whim for a famous bullfighter.

Such male arbitrariness cannot be tolerated in a woman and Carmen, a feminine Don Juan in her free sensuality, pays for her sexual independence with her life.

Men's traditional excuse for falling in love with a temptress is that she deploys supernatural powers. In Homer's poem *The Odyssey*, for example, the beautiful island sorceress Circe ensnared even the wily Odysseus, returning home from the wars of Troy. In mythology, the island with its temptress is often a metaphor for irresponsible pleasure — a sensual haven isolated from the outside world. The final threat — or promise — is that this idyll could become permanent: on another island, the charming nymph Calypso had it in her gift to offer Odysseus immortality.

Henri Matisse's Odalisque in Grey Trousers *depicts a
semi-naked female slave, reclining on a bed of cushions.*

THE BROKEN VOW

In P. H. Calderon's painting Broken Vows *a distraught woman overhears her lover flirting with another.*

Novels of the 19th century are littered with women jilted at the altar, or earlier, by seducers who never intended to keep their vows. Underlying these dramatic scenes was the fear of something far more common — the betrayal of love within marriage itself. The whole literature of love tells us that its vows are not like other promises. They are emotional, not rational, and based on the impulses of the heart — a notoriously unreliable organ. Even those who love faithfully for years are not immune from change. "Who could have foretold," asked W. B. Yeats, "that the heart would grow old?"

All true lovers deny the power of time to erode the strength and sincerity of their feelings. For them, the boast of Enobarbus in Shakespeare's *Antony and Cleopatra* carries absolute conviction: "Age cannot wither her, nor custom stale / Her infinite variety." However, in literature — and often in life — the joyous comedy of falling in love is matched by the tragedy of falling out of it.

Often a third party simply provides the catalyst for a failing relationship, yet adultery remains one of the most bitter reasons for breaking up. Penalties for it have traditionally been severe, especially for erring women who risked social disgrace or even death.

Many of the greatest love stories, like those of Tristan and Isolde, Rick and Ilse in *Casablanca* and Helen of Troy and Paris, involve dangerous triangles. One of the great paradoxes of love is that disloyalty to an old love may seem acceptable, even heroic, if it is for the sake of a new. The concept of a noble betrayal infuses the medieval tradition of courtly love, which clearly distinguishes between the vows of love and those of marriage. Yet what is seldom absent from any of these stories is the pervasive, insidious effect of guilt — the inescapable result of the broken vow.

In the 16th-century French painting
Woman Between Two Ages of Man,
*a woman removes the glasses from her elderly
husband, thus blinding him to her adultery
with a handsome young lover.*

THE QUARREL

Seemingly foolish and often explosive, the lovers' quarrel is an ancient rite for couples, a way of reiterating and recharging the love that they are in the midst of denying. "Lovers' quarrels," wrote the Roman playwright Terence, "are the renewal of love." The quarrel is flirtation in disguise, a sexually charged, verbal tussle which allows lovers to recreate the beginning of their love. "When with unkindness our love at a stand is / And both have punish'd ourselves with the pain, / Ah what a pleasure the touch of her hand is, / Ah what a pleasure to press it again," sighed John Dryden. At the end of Jane Austen's insightful novel *Pride and Prejudice*, Elizabeth Bennett actually promises to argue with Mr Darcy when married: "... it belongs to me to find occasions for teasing and quarrelling with you as often as may be."

Literature relishes the conflicts of magnificently noisy couples, for example the skirmishes of Stella and Stanley in Tennessee Williams' play *A Streetcar Named Desire*; the domestic tussles of Chaucer's Wife of Bath with her younger, much loved Jankyn; and the passionate taunts of Shakespeare's Antony and Cleopatra. Their quarrels contain an absurdity familiar to everyone who has found in the burnt dinner a peg on which to hang the real issue: is love still there?

Perhaps because young love is expected to blow hot and cold, age tends to dismiss its quarrels patronizingly as tiffs. However, tiffs in a relationship are rarely outgrown. Lovers continue to ambush each other with arguments into old age, possibly as a challenge to the tedium of perpetual harmony.

Lovers' quarrels can be dangerous. This woodcut by Masereel depicts a woman finding solace in the arms of another, leaving her lover bereft.

This complex manoeuvring is often essential to the survival of love itself. As Alain de Botton writes in his *Essays on Love*, we mistakenly cling "to the idea of a hermetic division between love and non-love, one that should be crossed only twice, at the beginning and end of a relationship — rather than commuted across daily, or hourly. There is an impulse to split love and hate apart, rather than to see them as legitimate responses to the many sides of a single person."

The mystery of the lovers' quarrel lies less in its beginning, often triggered by daily irritations or anxieties, than in its end, when apparently deep-seated anger can be dissolved with a joke or a single intimate glance. In Dorothy Parker's short story "The Lovely Leave", a young wife — aghast that her husband's stay has been cut from 24 hours to one — cannot prevent herself from quarrelling and reconciling with him every precious minute of their meeting. One moment, she is full of hurt and fury, the next: "He had hung his blouse and necktie neatly over a chair and he was unbuttoning his shirt. As she came in, he took it off. She looked at the beautiful brown triangle of his back. She would do anything for him, anything in the world."

The complex, often irrational fluctuation of our feelings promotes arguments in most close human relationships. However, the intensity of our emotional preoccupation with a partner gives such quarrels a much deeper, lasting significance. It may expose any fragility in a relationship with brutal clarity, startling both parties with the violence of the feelings that are revealed. Yet no affair of the heart can endure without the ability to weather an argument and to savour reconciliation — and love itself may well emerge stronger as a result.

In turning our back on someone we are both distancing ourselves from them and buying time to cover our emotions. In Dudley Hardy's A Slight Difference of Opinion *(left) an woman ignores her lover as he leaves. Similar body language is used in Emma Turpin's* The Talking Garden *(below).*

E.Turpin 93

THE PARTING

Sleeplessness is common when we are separated from the one we love. In this Indian miniature a lady is waiting through the night for her lover to return.

The anguish of lovers who cannot be together has been the inspiration for some of the most beautiful and enduring literature on love in the world. The simply expressed yearning of the anonymous poem, "Western Wind", written in the 16th century, provides a powerful emotional charge: "Western wind, when will thou blow, / The small rain down can rain? / Christ, if my love were in my arms / And I in my bed again!" A Chinese poem of the 8th century, "The River-Merchant's Wife: A Letter", also retains the freshness of verses written yesterday. The wife, who is only 16 and has been missing her husband for five months, feels such longing for him that even the sight of paired butterflies is a source of pain: "They hurt me. I grow older."

Schopenhauer, the philosopher, wrote that "every parting gives a foretaste of death", a perception particularly true of wartime partings, which are filled with anticipatory dread. "How long ago Hector took off his plume / Not wanting that his little son should cry / Then kisses his sad Andromache goodbye — / And now we three in Euston waiting-room." Frances Cornford's sober poem recognizes the appalling timelessness of such anguished farewells, and, in the allusion to the fated Trojan prince Hector and his widow, the heroism of those who have to endure them.

Willy Ronis's photograph Devant Chez Mestre, *taken in Paris
in 1948, shows a couple bidding each other a long good night,
having spent the evening together.*

THE LOVE-DEATH

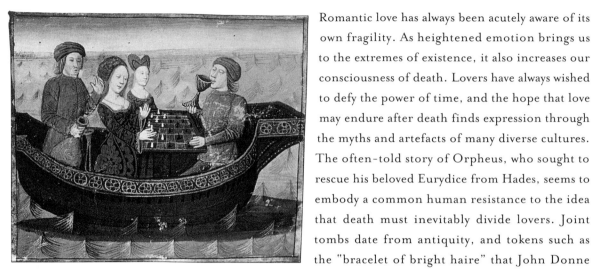

The tragic story of Tristan and Isolde is one of the most enduring medieval romances. Their love was fatally aroused by a magic potion which they unknowingly drank as Tristan escorted Isolde, his uncle's future bride, to her wedding. The lovers eventually died as a consequence of their forbidden passion.

Romantic love has always been acutely aware of its own fragility. As heightened emotion brings us to the extremes of existence, it also increases our consciousness of death. Lovers have always wished to defy the power of time, and the hope that love may endure after death finds expression through the myths and artefacts of many diverse cultures. The often-told story of Orpheus, who sought to rescue his beloved Eurydice from Hades, seems to embody a common human resistance to the idea that death must inevitably divide lovers. Joint tombs date from antiquity, and tokens such as the "bracelet of bright haire" that John Donne imagines tied around his arm after death symbolize the desire for lasting union. The poignancy of such gestures, and of love itself, lies in the contrast between what we know rationally and feel emotionally. We recognize mortality, but refuse to accept the extinguishing of emotions that once seemed infinite.

The 19th century enjoyed a romantic obsession with death, and the question of whether love could outlast it. A Christian religious faith offered hope to Elizabeth Barrett Browning, who wrote to her husband Robert: "I love thee with the breath / Smiles, tears, of all my life! - and, if God choose / I shall but love thee better after death." The prospect of death could assume a sensuous, if sometimes rather macabre, fascination, as in Victor Hugo's novel *Les Misérables*: "O, to lie together in the same tomb and sometimes caress with a finger tip in the shades; for me, that will suffice for eternity," Marius declares to his lover Cossette.

Lovers who choose to die together rather than survive alone have featured in tragic drama and opera for centuries. Often

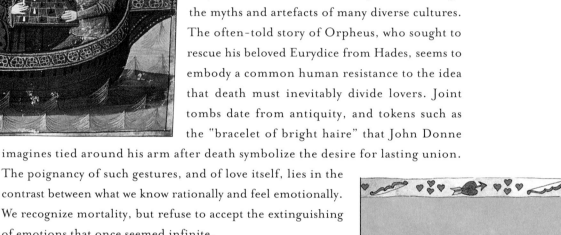

The sound of her silk skirt has stopped.
On the marble pavement, dusk grows.
Her empty room is cold and still.
Fallen leaves are piled against the doors.
Longing for that lovely lady,
How can I bring my aching heart to rest?

Wu Ti, 6th Han Emperor, 157–87 BC,
trs by Arthur Waley

their decision is based on a tragic misunderstanding, as in the deaths of Shakespeare's Romeo and Juliet or the lovers of Ovid's tale of Pyramus and Thisbe. The idea of the love-death is perfected in the Wagnerian *Liebestod* of Tristan and Isolde. The composer translated the medieval story of guilt-ridden love into an opera that celebrates the triumph of true love over death. As Tristan dies, Isolde — by a sheer effort of will — collapses dead over his body. The lovers achieve a union in death that, paradoxically, could never have been sustained in life.

The love-death theme expresses the emotional truth that life may seem insupportable without the loved one. Puccini's heroine Tosca, for example, chooses to leap to her death after realizing that her lover, Cavaradossi, has been executed. Even the gods of Greek myth take pity upon the anguish of the bereaved Alcyone, transforming her and her dead husband Ceyx into kingfishers who fly together over the waves.

The ancient practice of *suttee* in India provides a powerful example of love-death translated into social ritual. As proof of their grief and loyalty, Hindu wives were required to sacrifice themselves upon the funeral pyres of their husbands. In so doing they echoed the mythological immolation of Sati, the

first consort of the god Shiva, who was seen as the epitome of true wives.

Although few people actually die of love, the point of the archetype is that innumerable parted lovers have longed to die. There is also a deep-seated horror of letting an adored Other go into the afterworld alone. The desire to go hand-in-hand is irrational — but so are many impulses of passionate love.

This work by Alessandro Varotari depicts the story of Orpheus and his wife Eurydice. When Eurydice died, Orpheus sought her in Hades. He failed to win her back and was later killed by a band of women who were tired of his excessive grieving.

THE ONE AND ONLY

The Bride and Groom *by Marc Chagall depicts a young couple celebrating after their marriage.*

For centuries, the idea of exclusivity has held great emotional appeal for romantic love. Our different relationships in the real world prove that how we love, and whom, may alter over time. Yet the belief that we can truly love only once keeps a pervasive hold on the human imagination.

The concept of a "one and only" love is very ancient. It forms the central theme of the beautiful Song of Songs, in the Old Testament of the Bible. The book is unique and so mysterious that scholars have never agreed on who wrote it or what it means. It seems to be a dialogue between a king (supposedly Solomon) and a lovely Shulamite girl who longs to leave his harem to be reunited with her adored shepherd. The power and sweetness of its poetry insist that romantic love can never be divided, but must be devoted to one single other soul.

The literature of love has celebrated this idea ever since. Yet our emotions remain complex, elusive and fluid — what we love, what we feel and what we find lovable are all subject to change over time.

F. Scott Fitzgerald's poignant and powerful novel *The Great Gatsby* describes its hero's failure to understand this. Jay Gatsby's first love, Daisy, has married a rich man, and Jay spends years making himself even richer before he attempts, fatally, to replay the idealized romance of his youth. Only Nick, the narrator, realizes the ephemerality of Gatsby's illusions: "He had come a long way to this blue lawn, and his dream must have seemed so close that he could hardly fail to grasp it. He did not know that it was already behind him, somewhere back in that vast obscurity beyond the city, where the dark fields of the republic rolled on under the night."

*Committing ourselves to one person radically changes the way
we view our lives. In this painting by Emma Turpin a bride finds
herself in a new and strange land.*

THE WORLD WELL LOST

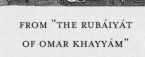

The bittersweetness of love is so finely balanced that we cannot always be sure that the happiness it brings will outweigh the pain. Many myths and fairytales confront this dilemma, perhaps most poignantly in Hans Christian Andersen's famous story of the little mermaid. Her sacrifices for love included leaving her own world, losing her voice and exchanging her tail for human feet – although each step she took felt as if she were treading on knives.

The little mermaid's sufferings were not over when she was united with her prince; he treated her kindly, but then married a human princess. Faced with the cruel choice of killing him or turning to sea foam, she nobly flung herself from his ship into the waves.

The power in the idea of a world well lost for love derives from the real-life exemplars who complement the literary theme. For the medieval world it was epitomized by the French lovers Abélard and Héloïse.

Peter Abélard, one of the greatest of 12th-century theologians, plunged into a passionate, illicit love affair with a brilliant pupil, Héloïse. She bore his child, after which Abélard, his career compromised, was emasculated by her vindictive uncle. From the convent which she entered (which was founded by Abélard), Héloïse wrote hundreds of letters to him. Their sentiments were remarkable for an age in which human love was morally subordinated to the love of God. "Not piety, only an order from you has delivered me up so young to the rigours of monastic life," she said. "God knows, I would not have hesitated to follow you or go before you into Hell if you had ordered me to do so." Despite their long separation, her

This 14th-century miniature depicts the lovers Peter Abélard and his pupil Héloïse. The couple are clearly still fascinated by each another, despite their religious orders and the cruelty they have both suffered for their love.

FROM "THE RUBÁIYÁT
OF OMAR KHAYYÁM"

Alas, that Spring should vanish with the Rose!
That Youth's sweet-scented Manuscript should close!
The Nightingale that in the Branches sang,
Ah, whence, and whither flown again, who knows!

Ah Love! could thou and I with Fate conspire
To grasp this sorry Scheme of Things entire,
Would not we shatter it to bits — and then
Re-mould it nearer to the Heart's Desire!

Edward Fitzgerald (1809–83)

life was dedicated to the love that she continued to feel for Abélard. When he died, his body was brought to Héloïse's convent for burial.

The strains inherent in putting love before everything else were explored by the great Russian writer Leo Tolstoy in his novel *Anna Karenina*. Its heroine, Anna, is a beautiful and charming woman whose dull married life is transformed by her passion for an equally attractive young officer, Count Vronsky. The social consequences of their transgression are quickly apparent — to be with her lover, Anna must abandon her adored child. Before long, Vronsky, who has himself given up his army career for Anna, begins to feel the unbearable pressure of his obligation to maintain love at the heightened level that justified these huge sacrifices. The relationship becomes increasingly unhappy, and Anna does not survive the bitterness of their first real quarrel. In depicting the affair's fatal outcome, Tolstoy reminds us that ultimately lovers can- not forget the real world in which they have to live.

This late 18th century painting from Rajasthan shows two lovers lying on a couch under a canopy. At such moments the cares of the real world disappear or become, for a time, insignificant.

BIBLIOGRAPHY

Barnstone, A. and W. (eds), *A Book of Women Poets*, New York: Schocken Books (1980).

Bergmann, M. S., *The Anatomy of Loving*, New York: Columbia University Press (1987).

Boase, R., *The Origin and Meaning of Courtly Love*, Manchester: Manchester University Press (1977).

Charter, R. (ed.), *A History of Private Life*, Cambridge, Mass.: Harvard University Press (1987).

Clayton, J., *Romantic Vision and the Novel*, Cambridge: Cambridge University Press (1987).

De Botton, A., *The Romantic Movement*, London: Macmillan (1994).

de la Mare, W., *Love (anthology)*, London: Faber (1943).

Duffy, M., *The Erotic World of Faery*, London: Hodder & Stoughton (1972).

Epton, N., *Love and the French*, London: Cassell (1959).

Epton, N., *Love and the Spanish*, London: Cassell (1961).

Fuller, J. (ed.), *The Chatto Book of Love Poetry*, London: Chatto & Windus (1990).

Fromm, E., *The Art of Loving*, London: Allen & Unwin (1957).

Gunn, A. M. F., *The Mirror of Love*, Lubbock: Texas Technical Press (1952).

Hagstrum, J. H., *The Romantic Body*, Knoxville: University of Tennessee Press (1986).

Hendrix, H., *Getting the Love You Want*, New York: Simon & Schuster (1992).

Hilton, T., *Keats and His World*, London: Thames & Hudson (1971).

Huot, S., *The Romance of the Rose*, Cambridge: Cambridge University Press (1993).

Kennedy, B., *Knighthood in the Morte d'Arthur*, Cambridge: D. S. Brewer (1985).

Kernberg, O., *Love Relations*, New Haven and London: Yale University Press (1995).

Kristeva, J., *Tales of Love*, New York: Columbia University Press (1987).

Lilar, S., *Aspects of Love*, London: Thames & Hudson trs by Jonathan Griffin (1965).

Lockridge, L. S., *The Ethics of Romanticism*, Cambridge:

Cambridge University Press (1989).

Lystra, K., *Searching the Heart*, New York: Oxford University Press (1989).

Morphod, M. P. O. and Lenardon, R. J. *Classical Mythology*, White Plains, NY: Longman (1995).

O'Brien, E., *Some Irish Loving*, London: Weidenfeld & Nicolson (1979).

Owen, David (compiler), *Seven Ages: Poetry for a Lifetime*, London: Michael Joseph (1992).

Owen, D. D. R., *Noble Lovers*, London: Phaidon (1975).

Stallworthy, J. (ed.), *The Penguin Book of Love Poetry*, London: Allen Lane (1973).

Stendhal, *Love*, London: Merlin Press translation (1957).

Tergit, G., *Flowers through the Ages*, London: Oswald Wolff (1961).

Turner, J., *Love Letters*, 975–1944, London: Cassell (1969).

Zeldin, T., *An Intimate History of Humanity*, London: Sinclair-Stevenson (1994).

INDEX

ACKNOWLEDGMENTS

I would like to thank the following people for their help: the editorial and design team at DBP and especially my editor Catherine Bradley; my sister Jody; Susan Collier; Simon Browne-Wilkinson; Ben Gibson and the staff at the London Library. I owe special thanks to Jack Tresidder, without whom this book would not have been written.

PICTURE CREDITS

Key:
BAL – Bridgeman Art Library
etA – e.t. Archive

The author and publishers would like to thank the following people, museums and photographic libraries for permission to reproduce their material. Every care has been taken to trace copyright owners. However, if we have omitted anyone we apologize and will, if informed, make corrections in any future edition.

p.1: British Library, London (BAL); p.2: © Emma Turpin; p.3: Wolseley Fine Arts, London © The Heirs of Eric Gill; p.4: © Celia Birtwell, London; p.5: © Emma Turpin; p.8: © Emma Turpin; p.9: Private Collection (Christie's Images); pp.10-11: © Celia Birtwell, London; p.11: Musée Cluny, Paris (Giraudon/BAL); p.12: *above* Louvre, Paris (BAL); p.12: *below* Borghese

Gallery, Rome (AKG London); p.13: Victoria & Albert Museum (BAL); p.14: Private Collection (BAL); p.16: British Library, London (BAL); p.17: *left* The Mansell Collection, London; p.17: *right* Wolseley Fine Arts, London © The Heirs of Eric Gill; p.18. © Emma Turpin; p.20: *left and right* Rose Castle, Cumbria (BAL); p.20: *centre* The Mansell Collection, London; p.20: *below* Museo Diocesano de Solsona Lerida (Index /BAL); p.21: Musée de Grenoble (etA); p.21: *right* Rose Castle, Cumbria (BAL); p.22: Private Collection (BAL); p.23: Victoria & Albert Museum, London (etA); p25: Phillips Fine Art Auctioneers, London (BAL) © ADAGP, Paris & DACS, London 1997; p.26: *above* Victoria & Albert Museum, London (BAL); p.26: *below* Fitzwilliam Museum, University of Cambridge (BAL); p.27: Private Collection (BAL); p.27: *right* British Museum, London; p.28: Private Collection (Christie's Images); p.29: Prado, Madrid (AKG London); p.30: British Library, London (BAL); p.31: *above* © Emma Turpin; p.31: *below* Bibliothèque Nationale, Paris (BAL); p.33: © Thurston Hopkins/Portfolio Ltd, London; pp.34-5: © Thurston Hopkins/Portfolio Ltd, London; p.36: *above* British Library, Paris (BAL); p.36: *below* Musée Condé, Chantilly (AKG London/Erich Lessing); p.36 and

p.37: *details* Musée Mobilier National, Paris (Giraudon/BAL); p.37: Louvre, Paris (AKG London/ Erich Lessing); p.38: *above* Private Collection; p.38: *left* National Gallery, London; p 38: *right* Kunsthistorisches Museum, Vienna (BAL); p.39: © Emma Turpin; p.40: Museo Civico Ascoli Piceno (etA); p.41: National Gallery, Budapest (etA); p.42: © Europa Verlag, Zurich, pp.42-3 Borough of Southwark, London (BAL); p.43: *left* Private Collection; p.43: *right* University of Liverpool Art Gallery (BAL); p.44: Wolseley Fine Arts, London © The Heirs of Eric Gill; p.45: © Emma Turpin; p.47: Wolseley Fine Arts, London © The Heirs of Eric Gill; pp.48-9: © Trevor Watson/Portfolio Ltd, London; p.50: © Emma Turpin; p.52: Victoria & Albert Museum, London (AKG London); p.52 and p.53: *details* Kupferstichkabinett, Berlin (AKG London); p.53: Galerie d'Art Moderne, Paris (etA) © Succession H. Matisse/DACS, 1997; p.54: The Wallace Collection, London (BAL); p.55: Wolverhampton Art Gallery (BAL); p.56: *left* Victoria & Albert Museum, London (BAL); p.56: *right* National Gallery, London; p.56: *below* © Emma Turpin; p.57: Roy Miles Gallery, London (BAL); p.58: *left* National Gallery, London

(BAL); p.58. *right* Private Collection (David Alexander); p.59: National Gallery of Art, Washington D.C. (BAL) © Succession Picasso/ DACS, 1997; p.60: Musée Cluny, Paris (Giraudon/BAL); p.61: Hirshhorn Museum & Sculpture Garden, Smithsonian Institute (Gift of Joseph Hirshhorn Foundation), Washington DC (AKG London); p.62: *left* Musée Bonnat, Bayonne (etA); p.62: *right* © Europa Verlag, Zurich; p.63: Lutherhalle, Wittenberg (AKG London); p.64. Private Collection (etA); p.65: Fine Art Society, London (etA); p.67: © Roderick A. Field/Portfolio Ltd, London; pp.68-9: © Thurston Hopkins/Portfolio Ltd, London; p.70: Musée Condé, Chantilly (BAL); p.71: Private Collection (BAL), p.72: *left* Private Collection (etA) © ADAGP, Paris & DACS, London 1997; p.72: *right* Christopher Wood Gallery, London (BAL); p.73: Ca' Rezzonico, Venice (etA); p.74: *left* Palazzo Ducale, Mantua (BAL); p.74: *right* Musée d'Orsay, Paris (etA); p.75: *above* Belvedere Galerie, Vienna (AKG London); p.75: *below* Bibliothèque Nationale, Paris (BAL); pp.76-7: © Emma Turpin; p.77: *right* Bibliothèque Nationale, Paris (BAL); p.79: Wolseley Fine Arts, London © The Heirs of Eric Gill; pp.80-81: © Willy Ronis/Rapho; p.82: © Emma Turpin;

TEXT CREDITS